THE UNCOMFORTABLE ZONE

THE UNCOMFORTABLE ZONE

Down From The Mountains

A book about growing up in War by the author of
The 'Comfort Zone Growing Up in Appalachia'

KENNETH A. LUIKART

XULON PRESS

Xulon Press
2301 Lucien Way #415
Maitland, FL 32751
407.339.4217
www.xulonpress.com

Unless otherwise indicated, Scripture quotations taken from the King James Version (KJV)–*public domain.*

Printed in the United States of America.

ISBN-13: 9781545629932

CONTENTS

PREFACE

This is the fiftieth anniversary of the beginning of the long ten-year war called the Vietnam War by Americans and the American War by the Vietnamese. Fifty years can cloud a memory or embellish a fact, yet some things are burned into the mind like a bad accident. It's very difficult to admit we should not have entered that war. I agree, to a point, that looking back it is easier to condemn than to understand.

Australia, New Zealand, Thailand, and South Korea were into the war, as we were. These soldiers were supportive and great allies to work with. Obviously, they had more at stake if you consider the domino effect — one country falling after another and, to an extent, this happened. Laos, Cambodia and parts of Indonesia, as well as internal struggles in Thailand and South Vietnam, were engulfed or at least harassed by communism.

It's been fifty years now, half a century, and new documents and stories will be unveiled. This will give us more insight into the strategic ins and outs of Vietnam. This account is, to the best of my knowledge, what I thought happened while I was deployed. It may need more clarification, additions, or corrections from peers. Embellishment comes from time, and what I thought happened.

To my kids and grandchildren and their children, I hope this account will prove that Vietnam was a full-scale war, at Division and Corps level, on both sides, that it was truly a war, and that no war is glory, nor are there winners. Political leaders are the only ones who claim victory, or blame poor intelligence for defeat. For those of us who served in war and survived, there is guilt, anxiety, difficulty in merging back into society, hatred of one's own country, distrust, anger, post-traumatic stress disorder, dreams, uneasiness at O'dark thirty, and scars — visible scars and invisible scars. It is what a war leaves with young men who survive.

My book is dedicated to all men who have served in our military. They will relate, better or worse, to these stories. But specifically my book is dedicated to Specialist 5th Class Harold Douglas (Doug) Biller from Silver Springs, Maryland, who volunteered to go to pick up needed supplies and left in a convoy. He was killed at Nui Dat by a command detonated land mine on 25 February, 1969. He was a brother in arms, belonging to the Army Security Agency.

Soldiers' Statement of Faith — "The Warriors Psalm" — Psalm 91 (KJV)

1 He that dwelleth in the secret place of the most High shall abide under the shadow of the Almighty.
2 I will say of the Lord, He is my refuge and my fortress: my God; in Him will I trust.
3 Surely He shall deliver thee from the snare of the Fowler, and from the noisome pestilence.
4 He shall cover thee with His feathers, and under His wings shalt thou trust; His truth shall be thy shield and buckler.
5 Thou shalt not be afraid for the terror by night; nor for the arrow that flieth by day;
6 Nor for the pestilence that walketh in darkness; nor for the destruction that wasteth at noonday.
7 A thousand shall fall at thy side, and ten thousand at thy right hand; but it shall not come nigh thee.
8 Only with thine eyes shalt thou behold and see the reward of the wicked.

9 Because thou hast made the Lord, which is my refuge, even the most High, thy Habitation;

10 There shall no evil befall thee, neither shall any plague come nigh thy dwelling.

11 For He shall give His angels charge over thee, to keep thee in all thy ways.

12 They shall bear thee up in their hands, lest thou dash thy foot against a stone.

13 Thou shalt tread upon the lion and adder: the young lion and the dragon shalt thou trample under feet.

14 Because He hath set His love upon me, therefore will I set Him on high, because He hath known my name.

15 He shall call upon me, and I will answer Him, and honour Him.

16 With long life will I satisfy Him, and shew Him my salvation.

Chapter 1:

LOST INNOCENCE

The heat was stifling. Overhead, a ceiling fan spun in a gyro motion. It was hanging by three wires and had no base with which to attach it to the ceiling. The sweat rolled off my body as I climbed into bed on the top rack. It was late and quiet on the main street of Cholon, the Chinese section of Saigon, Republic of Vietnam. This was the famous St. George Hotel the VC bombed only months earlier. Now it was my temporary home until I found a more suitable hotel before going to work.

I had just arrived in Saigon from the 303rd Radio Research Battalion (303rd RRBn). My next move would be working in a unit, or detachment, with an Army Security Agency (ASA), somewhere within Vietnam. We arrived with no top secret code word or Special Security Background Investigation (SSBI) clearances. This meant we couldn't work in the Operations Center because it was a top secret facility, and we only had secret clearances. That was a mistake. The Army was trying to fix a huge turnover in Combat Order of Battle Specialists, and we were chosen, all twelve of us, to fill those slots, but none of us were cleared for Top Secret Crypto Intelligence.

At battalion headquarters, the 303rd RRBn at Long Binh, they introduced us to pure fluoride toothpaste, probably Crest. We were led to a huge square sink. In front of us was a toothbrush and toothpaste with fluoride. The sergeant barked orders at us "remove the cap" and "brush those teeth vigorously in a vertical motion," and we were not allowed to spit until told to do so. That came several minutes after everyone had finished. Then we all spit and kept the toothpaste, and the toothbrush, stuffing them in our pockets. The US Army had pushed Crest toothpaste on us since basic training.

At battalion headquarters, they taught me how to clean out the latrines. For those of you who have had no military experience, a latrine is a slit trench or a bathroom. Slit trenches are like an outside toilet without any flushing water and always full of flies. This was a very dirty job requiring gloves and a hook to pull out the bottom half of a fifty-five-gallon drum. You also had a can of diesel fuel.

Every Vietnam veteran knows of this job and has probably completed this task with the same grim determination. We poured diesel fuel into the drum, full of excrement, then lit the mixture with a match and a newspaper. The black fuel wafted into the air circulating around and around, filling the skies with the most nauseating smell of burning human waste. It's a smell that has that sweet sickening aroma that can never be forgotten, and a black cloud that could be seen for miles around.

Ah, the smells in Vietnam, especially Saigon, are too numerous to list. Our olfactory nerves picked up all of these repulsive smells instantly. A smell of spent diesel fuel from a vehicle, open sewers, and the misty, musty rot of mildew and sweat. These are smells you always remember. I was not one to put down another country, but these smells to an American from Appalachia were vibrant and hard to escape.

We left Japan for Vietnam on my trip over and arrived at Bien Hoa Air Base, Vietnam, on August 17, 1968. We were rushed off the plane and made to sit in a trench until the 'all clear' siren. Bien Hoa, my future home, was hit yet again with 122mm rockets. This airbase was the most heavily bombed during the war.

After in processing at Bien Hoa, we were loaded onto buses and sent to Long Binh, about seven miles away. On the way over, I spied a woman just stop, pull down her pants in the rice paddy, and squat. I told the boy beside me, "We ain't in Kansas no more." He agreed.

We stayed in tents at Long Binh where we practiced our duck and cover skills yet again. Charley VC (Viet Cong—or enemy) was busy. Usually the local sapper battalions (commando units) hit our bases with mortars and rockets once or twice a week. It would not be my last encounter with incoming missiles.

The ride to Saigon, three days later, to the 90th Replacement Battalion was bitter sweet. We were surrounded by thousands of mopeds, motorcycles, and small cars. We sat in the back of an open Deuce and a half (2 ½ ton truck) exposed to the open air like apples for the picking. Every motorcycle that zoomed close by put fear and a little dread in our hearts. We kept thinking, *Was this guy a VC, or was he a nice person?* We had no clue. Frankly, we felt very naked without firearms.

We were girl watching, too. That had a soothing effect until our truck driver yelled at us about "Saigon Sally." Saigon who? We asked. "Saigon Sally is a beautiful girl, half French and Vietnamese. She rides around in a white Aou Dai (Vietnamese dress) and smiles at you, and then she kills you with a pistol or throws a grenade at you." I thought for a minute, *How many pretty girls are riding around us?* It seemed like millions. That took away our last ounce of fun and put more dread on us until we reached the Cholon district. It was probably a safer place to rest and bunk than anywhere else in the city. Rockets seldom hit here; however, there was the occasional sapper attack on a hotel where GIs were staying. It would be my luck that my hotel, the St. George, was still recovering from the earlier attack.

The fan continued to gyrate, and to keep my mind thinking of something other than dying by a faulty fan. I pondered my life. I turned eighteen in high school, and that meant I registered for a draft card. My birthday fell one day short of putting me in the first grade at age six. So I waited a year and began my school career five months before my seventh birthday. Draft cards in 1966 were a little more important than a social security card. Unless you were working, you seldom worried about it. Even if it was in your pocket from age sixteen, it did not carry the weight of a draft card. That card could change your life forever. Every young boy eighteen years old knew the future looked very scary. The draft card could get you into carnival shows meant for adults, sometimes to the dismay of the young invitees. Also, a draft card meant you could drink a beer back then. I didn't like liquor, but agreed with the adage: if you're old enough to fight, you're old enough to vote and drink a beer.

We didn't have a drug problem in school in those days, although there might have been a drinking problem. Nor did we fear for our lives when we were visiting downtown Nitro. It seems that the world went to pieces sometime after 1966 — yes, sometime after graduating high school in 1966. Changes come in many forms. Most changes are subtle; others are quick and harsh. I cannot put my finger on exactly what occurred, but 1967 seems to be the turning point in our nation. Maybe it was LSD or cocaine or heroin, but something changed young people across our nation. Movies changed, and were more graphic and sexual in nature. Changes were coming to America, big changes, and I was right in the middle of them. Truly, our innocence was lost.

Maybe the turning point was earlier in the 60's during a presidential speech by Lyndon Baines Johnson. While on a family camping trip to Holly River State Park, West Virginia, in the summer of 1964, we were making sandwiches for lunch. On the radio I heard President Johnson mention the Gulf of Tonkin resolution. Until this speech, Vietnam was John F. Kennedy's war, a Special Forces (Green Beret) war. After this resolution was passed, the United States turned the Vietnam counter-insurgency conflict into a North Vietnamese–United States war.

I was always inclined to join the army, but I never dreamed the conflict in Vietnam would become a full-fledged war, a war the country would not recognize as a real fight for our survival. No, Vietnam was a million miles away to most Americans. Ten years later, our nation was drained, and we flew away in helicopters to avoid the misery of leaving millions of Vietnamese to the whims of the Communists, either execution or prison camps.

I was busy trying to graduate from high school in 1966 and decided to earn my tuition for college by working at A. W. Cox's Department Store. Mr. Tyson had called the school and asked for the names and phone numbers of two very honest students. Mrs. Willow, our counselor, gave him Boo Nelson's and my names. That's how I was asked to work for Cox's Department Store. I started off at a whopping $1.00 per hour.

I worked the menswear and shoe departments. Back in 1966 and 1967, women and men, actually wanted their feet measured. I would be lying if I said I hated that part of selling shoes. I loved sitting down and taking a woman's foot and placing it on the metal foot measure to get length and width. I was pretty good at selling shoes, men's clothes, belts, pants, and suits. After a few months, at age eighteen, I was a pretty good salesman.

Once a month, we were given the task of mopping and waxing all the floors in Cox's store. Our boss would lock us up in the store, and Boo and I would work all night sweeping, mopping, and waxing the floors. This came with a few hazards.

One night we were about half finished. Boo went to move a huge double tier of dresses, and it tipped on him. I rushed in to help, and I was surprised at the weight of this display rack. It was about to fall, and I heard Boo laughing, a bad sign because that was his hysterical laugh he guffawed when things were going very wrong. Finally, we managed to right the stand, but it drained every ounce of strength out of us. Display racks were the heaviest objects to move and always caused us problems.

Upstairs, above Cox's Department Store, was the surreal land of "storage." Here was a dimly lit huge area, the same size as the store below, with things strewn here and there and piled high with display stands, boxes of office supplies, tables, and mannequins. These were both male and female and were painted white. This was a scary and surreal sight to behold. Unclothed, hands reaching out, staring at nothing, they always gave me the creeps going up there. Whenever supplies came to the store, Boo and I would carry box after box up the steps to the storage area. Eventually we would lug them back downstairs and help sort out shoes, dresses, and what-not, to all the departments.

To earn extra money for college I washed windows throughout Nitro. One of the sweet older ladies, who worked in Cox's, kept me busy keeping her windows spotless. She was a kind lady that worked in the women's department. I had given up my paper route and was employed part-time at Cox's. As the summer wore on and college was on the horizon, I needed more hours. So, I went to work for an engineering survey crew at "Home Engineering."

I worked as a rod-and-chain man. I learned the correct way to chain distances in mountainous terrain, which is difficult if you don't know what you're doing. The big television towers on top of the hill above Jefferson City were a large project I helped survey and prepare for installation. I made 10 percent of what our boss was paid, which was not too bad of a deal. If we surveyed a yard for two hundred dollars, I made 10 percent of it. If we did three yards in a day, I could make sixty dollars. That was very good money in 1966.

While working for Home Engineering, the boss received special passes to see President Johnson dedicate the Summersville Dam. He was able to find two more passes and took his entire crew to the Summersville Dam for the dedication. I was fortunate enough to sit in the press gallery up front, near the stage. President Johnson finally took the podium and began his speech with a very funny story.

Today we are dedicating the Summersville Dam. It's a West Virginia tradition to name the dam after the closest town it's built near. The closest town to this dam is Gad, West Virginia. Now, no one in the state wanted to call this the Gad Dam, so they chose the next closest city, Summersville. Now can you imagine the newspaper headline if a woman from up the road at Big Ugly, West Virginia, was to drown in that lake? The headlines would read "Big Ugly Woman drowns in Gad dam lake!"

Lyndon Baines Johnson; Summersville, West Virginia Dam Dedication, 1967

Well, that was a story that made me want to roll on the ground laughing. He had a great sense of humor and was an interesting speaker (Speech by Lyndon Baines Johnson; Summersville West Virginia Dam Dedication, 1967).

Since high school, my heart was always into forestry. I heard about working the Oak Wilt Project from a friend who knew I wanted to be a forest ranger. I went up to the state capital and placed an application with the Department of Natural Resources, State of West Virginia. I was surprised that I received an immediate response. I went for an interview and was hired immediately and was looking forward to this job, even though it ended in September of 1966, prior to winter.

My dad took me to work in Charleston for a while until I was able to catch a ride every day from a fellow worker who lived in the town of Hurricane. Our days started early, about 8:00 a.m., and ended at dark. These were very long days, but I earned a dollar an hour! Our daily work ended when we came back to the office in a very large two-story house near the capital building.

Oak Wilt is a serious disease that enters into the vascular system of a tree and chokes it to death. Many states have different approaches to eradicating or fighting Oak Wilt. Pennsylvania used to cut everything down around the oak, including the tree itself and either burn it or remove it. West Virginia decided on the "tree girdle" method.

Aircraft flew at a low level over the mountains and hunted for changing foliage in the late summer. The crown of the tree would turn a golden yellow as it was dying and dropped its leaves. Oaks are the last trees to drop leaves for fall. They would mark it with toilet paper, then mark its location on a topographic map and bring it back in to the main office. The next day, each two-man crew was given maps and trees for a specific area. I would travel all over West Virginia looking for those trees that represented that "dot" on a map. Down around

Logan and southern West Virginia, the mountains were extremely steep. Slippery slate, abandoned coal mine shafts, and steep grades all added a dimension of difficulty to finding that tree. In addition, the maps we were working off of were surveyed in 1918, with a scale of one inch equals one mile. This meant that sometimes a mountain peak on the map didn't exist. And that added drama to hunting down a tree stuck between two hollers with no way to get to it but to hike.

Once we were in the vicinity we would look for the marked tree. Aircraft marked each tree with toilet paper, or adding machine paper, thrown from a slow-flying aircraft. The paper would wind all through the limbs and spin around and make a great marking tool. Another sign we were at the right spot was the amount of golden oak leaves all over the ground. The tree was dying, and we were there to help it die quicker.

Our objective was to create a situation where the tree would die much quicker causing it to create hypoxylon, a form of mold that grew and thrived off of Oak Wilt, thus killing the tree so that it could not spread the Wilt. There was black and gray hypoxylon, and we noted the difference on trees we revisited a year after they were treated.

On one of our treks into the hills of southern West Virginia, the crew climbed a steep hillside with slippery slate underfoot. The grade was so steep we reached for the bottoms of small trees above our heads to pull ourselves up and then repeat the process again. Eventually, we found an old timber road that led to the top of the hill, and over the ridge line to the other side of the hill, halfway down, we spotted adding machine paper wound all through the branches. The paper wound up and down and around and around until the roll hit the ground. The golden leaves littering the ground gave evidence this was our tree.

We broke into individual jobs. One member began surveying the site for additional infected trees, another began taking notes and observations, and a third was about to use the ax on the tree to "quick kill" the oak in order to produce the good hypoxylon fungus that ate the wilt.

We used two-headed "Pennsylvania" axes. We sharpened both sides of the ax, and they were extremely sharp. The ax man had just removed the protective shield when the note taker was about to stand up and change positions. The ax man had drawn back to take a good swing when the ax cut the note taker two inches deep into the web of his hand. Blood began to pour out, and instantly they realized he was injured. We stopped the bleeding and bandaged his hand. Now we needed to hike back out and take him to a doctor. As far as I know, it was the only serious injury to anyone that summer, and we worked on about three to four trees a day. Unfortunately, several years later, an Oak Wilt spotter plane crashed into a mountainside in southern West Virginia, killing all on board. These men were truly heroes in my mind for their accuracy in spotting and marking trees in rough terrain.

I love traveling through southern West Virginia, south of Huntington, near Wayne County. We traveled narrow roads that wound through farmland framed by large hills on both sides of the road. Down in the valley, between the hills, was a broad, flat area good for farming. Houses were painted white with green trim. House after house was painted this beautiful color, and I remember how clean the farms appeared.

One day at lunch time we were very close to Lousia, Kentucky, and my supervisor took me over to Louisa to eat lunch so I could say I had visited Kentucky. That was a big deal to me as I had not traveled very far from Nitro growing up, except to visit relatives in Virginia. We traveled into steep mountainous areas, down near Van and Uneeda, West Virginia, where it was no easy feat to hike to the summit of the mountains located in southern West Virginia. We traveled down to Logan and over near Beckley and as far west as Fayette county and places like Mossy, Sharon, and Boomer, West Virginia. This job prepared me for a future in forestry with Union Camp Corporation.

That fall of 1966, I entered West Virginia State College and prepared myself for a career in forestry. The problem was, my guidance counselor at WVSC signed me up in a "premed" criteria and heaped eighteen semester hours on my back. Since I was a weak student with poor study habits, I was destined to fail. It was a chapter of my life that I am not proud of, but I think it's important for all young people to realize you will carry college failure with you all your life. The F never goes away.

At least I made an A in military history. This would help with my college grade-point average. I enjoyed my time with my ROTC buddies and enjoyed our outdoor exercises. During 1967, we visited Fort Bragg, North Carolina. The Special Forces (SF) instructors showed us how to get a chicken to calm down by crossing its wings. Then they immediately twisted off its head and held it upside down draining out the blood into a military tin cup. Each student was required to take one swig of the blood to taste its salty flavor, realizing that every part of a chicken should be eaten, including the blood. Growing up in a family that did not eat chicken, this was truly a challenge. While at Fort Bragg, we visited a drop zone and witnessed an air drop from a C130. In addition, we were given the SF briefing, similar to the one given in the movie *The Green Beret* starring John Wayne. This was probably the beginning of my military career.

Chapter 2

LEARNING THE HAND SLAP–1967

I paid my way, in full, into West Virginia State College, located in the town of Institute, West Virginia. Institute is a place, a city, not an asylum! I paid for college, but didn't have enough money for a driver's license or to buy a car. So, I rode to college with my dad early in the morning and rode the bus or bummed a ride home in the evenings.

If you stand up for your rights, those values your parents instill in you, you're destined for bad grades. It is true that if you like a subject, you probably will ace it. If you don't like the subject or the teacher will not explain things in detail, then you're probably going to fail.

Our social studies (what I call it) teacher lost me the day he encouraged all students to put aside what your parents taught you and drift away into new and more exciting adventures. This was foreign to me. I was raised a pretty sheltered young man. I guess you could say I was not the big man on campus at Nitro High School. But, you are what you are, and I didn't like this class. I think I got a C in that class.

I managed to squeak out a strong D in German, an A in military science, and two F's in zoology and trigonometry. Now my bad study habits were catching up to me. I was paying the price for throwing the books on the bed and going outside to hit the hillside and go hike or climb rocks. I have always received C grades in English. It is surprising that I have the ability to think clearly enough to write a book.

When abortion was discussed in English, I argued for those values my parents gave me. I didn't like abortions; it was killing a small human being with a soul. God gave us that human being, and it wasn't right to take its life. However, I was overwhelmed by female classmates who wanted abortion advocate laws. Speak your mind and move on was a good policy in that class because the professor usually zeroed in on you personally. My views were detrimental to passing his English class.

Zoology was a disaster when we began to study the theory of evolution, a theory I have never totally bought into. The teacher gave me an A for lab work. I did 100 percent of all labs and field work assigned. As a matter of fact, I was the only student to complete 100 percent of all field work. But I did not test well on the theory of evolution.

During a class on how clams became crabs, I had to ask the question. I raised my hand, and finally she called on me. I asked, "When the very first clam grew a claw, did it know it was a claw? Did he or she know how to eat with it? Or, did it think it could use it to push itself along the ocean floor?" She would ask back, "What are you talking about? This took millions of years to occur." I raised my hand, "But, I mean, when the very first claw appeared, very first one, did the clam think it was a clam or a crab? Was the clam scared to death with this strange appendage sticking out or did it accept it as part of evolution and try to grow more?" She was not happy with me. And for every species jump, she got the same question. "When did a human know it wasn't a monkey? I mean when did the first human say, I am man and not one of those ugly baboons? Did the first man think 'Do I need a hammer and a nail?' instantly; or did it miss its tail?" And thus, because of my hardhead-edness, I failed in all my subsequent ventures into college. Those F grades followed me throughout all of my future college years.

The bright spot of zoology happened when a small lamb fell from a truck onto the main highway and wandered over near the zoology building. While an argument took place about what to do with the poor thing, I chimed in. I knew somebody that might want that lamb. The instructor said, "Okay, Ken, if you're going to take care of it, then you can take it home." So I arranged a ride home, holding a lamb in my lap. When I got home, I took it to my neighbor next door, named Doc, and I begged him to keep it. "Doc, don't you think old Dick needs a companion to browse the hillside with?" At first he was adamant—no. Eventually he relented. For many, many years afterward, he always reminded me that I brought him that blasted sheep, and it had remained a pain in the neck ever since. The fact that every time he entered the pens to feed animals that sheep butted him in the butt might have been the reason he hated that sheep.

If I had learned to study, I might have had a better chance in college. But I loved to go outside and run the hills. Throwing books on the bed, I hit the door until suppertime usually exploring the hillside for new emerging springs, or new animal trails. I wouldn't come home until Dad whistled for David and me. I had a desk, but seldom used it. I tried the kitchen table, but it was too busy with traffic and supper preparation. I asked Dad several times to help me with algebra or trigonometry. Dad was very good at math, and he could sometimes solve those problems with pure logic. But, for many of those trig problems, knowing the formulas and how to solve for unknowns was the secret. I did not become math proficient until later after Vietnam.

I had some ROTC Special Forces training in college. Major Neal was our student commander. He had a great sense of humor, and I even invited him to visit the house for dinner during Thanksgiving, 1966. I hoped my brothers would behave, but with them you never knew.

Years ago, we went to visit Mom's good friend, Frieda Kelly, for thanksgiving. My dad does not like chicken. He complained all afternoon about going to a dinner where they were serving chicken. "It's a dirty bird," Daddy declared. "I've seen them eat stuff off the ground that is dirty, and I don't like eating chicken." Off to Thanksgiving dinner we went with Dad grumbling and Mom reminding him to be quiet. We arrived at Frieda's and immediately were seated for dinner. Frieda had fixed golden brown chicken and a carrot casserole, sprinkled with salt and pepper. My brother sat on his hands as Mom fixed his plate. "There, now when you clean your plate, you'll get desert," she said. My brother insisted, "I'm not eating that." He pointed at the chicken leg. "Daddy said chickens are dirty, momma." Then he pointed at the carrots, "And, look momma, those carrots have dirt on them." My mother, embarrassed and mad, smacked him and demanded he eat or else! He ate his meal.

During the academic year, one of the games we played in Reserve Officer Training Corps (ROTC) was "the four-man open-hand slap." Four students sat down on the ground with knees touching. Across from you was a student in the "on guard" position with his hands up. To your left was a student, and to the right a third student. On command you were free to slap any other student in the face while protecting your own jaw from being slapped. The decisions came quick and sometimes spontaneous. If you went to slap the man across from you, you got whacked from the right or the left. If you let your guard down to smack the man to your left, you got smashed in the face from the man in front of you. This was our favorite game.

I helped set up a field exercise in Nitro, at the old abandoned golf course at the end of 21st Street. This was before Ridenour Lake was built. I helped set up a field exercise that spanned several hundred acres across the undulating hills and a creek. It was a perfect place for maneuvers, and I remember helping belt-feed a 30 caliber water-cooled machine gun. I'm sure it was Korean War vintage. We used some homemade hand grenades, but after several went off, Sergeant Major Holland said, "No more!" I loved setting up those ambushes and acting like the Viet Cong.

Above St. Albans we practiced some tactical games with the junior and senior members of the ROTC program. In one scenario, we were well briefed by Cadet Major Neil, our Special Forces ROTC commander. We would attack the "enemy" and have a violent and quick firefight. Withdraw over the ridge top and wait only five minutes, then come roaring back and try to overrun their brief victory back slapping. It worked so perfect that they yelled "foul" and no fair. But what we taught these future officers was a valuable lesson; Charlie

VC does not play by the rules. They are devious and mean. I think we proved our point.

On Saturdays, we would run five miles and then practice normal infantry drills for hours. We learned how fire teams move in an infantry squad, how to hit the ground and roll, coming up firing, and a lot of hand-to-hand combat training. Our instructors were trained in street fighting. Similar to Jujitsu, the hand stance was classic street fighting. We learned how to parry a rifle with a bayonet coming at you bare handed, and how to kill someone from behind. All of this training was geared toward Vietnam. All our tactics and training was preparing us for Vietnam.

I was one of only three freshmen chosen to go to summer camp to provide the junior and senior ROTC members a token enemy force to fight in the woods of northern West Virginia. This training helped familiarize me with the army, so it wasn't quite the culture shock it could have been when I joined in 1968.

One evening we set up an ambush along a trail that followed a valley floor. The scenario called for at least a platoon-sized unit dismount on the main road and the set up of a combat patrol up the valley just before dusk. Four of us were hiding on the military crest, just below a major highway, overlooking the valley. From our vantage point, we could faintly see the column moving up the valley in combat formation. Staggered left and right, with about ten to twenty feet between each soldier, the column wound its way past us.

Our game plan was simple. At about the halfway point, or where the "enemy" commander and radio man were located, we would attack vigorously and then pull back to the road and run to the rear of the column and descend back downhill to attack their formation from the rear. We were camouflaged and quiet as the platoon meandered below us. The enemy platoon looked impressive in its combat formation. At about the formation's midpoint, our leader opened fire. All of us emptied our M1 rifles and pulled out quickly, heading uphill and reloading on the run. We hit the top of the hill, turned right, and were following the road toward the "enemy's" rear to conduct a second attack on the rear of the column. Then the unexpected happened. We didn't think about local civilian traffic on that lonely road. Sure enough, here came a pickup truck lumbering toward us. We hit the honeysuckle and buried ourselves in vines, but unfortunately, the driver of the pickup saw one us.

The truck slowed about a hundred yards behind us. It pulled over to the side of the road and stopped. We were breathing heavily, and one of my buddies, a black student from Pennsylvania, was lying near me. I whispered, "They're coming toward us; what are we going to do?" He snorted, "Well, I only know one thing to do." He stood up and unloaded his M1 carbine at the civilians! Of course these were just blanks, but the two men coming at us didn't know that. They stopped dead in their tracks and ran for the truck. Doors slammed, and the truck sped off downhill away from us. We turned and ran toward the back of the column and slipped downhill.

By now, we had missed our second opportunity to attack the enemy platoon. So we shadowed them for about a half mile. We eventually met up with the other team on a ridge top overlooking the military camp at Clifftop. Off to our left and below us in the valley, emergency lights were blinking brightly in the darkness. We knew the police had stopped at both the point of departure for the enemy platoon and at the spot where we fired on the civilians. We were scared to death. Not sure if they were going to press charges, come looking for us, or what was going to happen, we stayed put until late that night.

At about 10:00 p.m., we came in from the dark and secured our weapons in the weapons vault. Sergeant Major Holland was there waiting on us. All eight of us were standing at ease when he finally explained to us what had happened. The cops had stopped and talked with our commanding officer and Sergeant Major Holland. They explained to them that there was a large exercise going on and that sometimes it spilled over into the local area. The cops smiled, said, "No problem," and left. We were off the hook.

I was doing great in ROTC and physical fitness. I was doing fair in English, even though the teacher was constantly on me for my opinionated attitude. After a very inauspicious first year in college, I ended up with a 1.67 grade average. I did not receive a notice from the college or my adviser. Nothing was sent to the house to my parents. Needless to say, I was booted out of West Virginia State College! They put me on a year's probation; unfortunately, it was my one-way ticket to war. Because I was kicked out of college, I became a member of the US Army less than six months after my summer training at Clifftop.

What did I expect? I didn't study. Instead I played card games or pool at the Student Union. I did little homework and did not study. I got what I deserved, except I never received the letter of failure from the school. No, I didn't receive anything in the mail saying, "You are failing or you have failed or you are a dummy; come talk to your school counselor. No, I think they were tired of me, and they quietly let me stand in line that next September, 1967, for many hours.

Moving up slowly and tiresomely, it took me almost four hours to reach the registrar's desk. There in front of all my peer group, friends, and acquaintances, I was told you are a failure and that you get to go home. You could have knocked me over with a feather. I remember that long, lonesome day of standing in line and getting axed at the end. I will not forgive that school for its oversight, or perhaps, callous treatment of a young person. Some will argue this did not happen, but this is exactly what happened that day.

Most people only know I disappeared from school. I didn't talk to anyone, never said a word to anyone. I walked to the front of the school near the main highway. Across the highway was the bus stop for Nitro, but instead of taking the bus, I began to walk. I wasn't thumbing a ride, I wasn't going to ride the bus, I was walking. I past Carbide Institute Plant and on toward East Nitro and Sattes Circle, I walked. I had a million things go through my mind. I had always pulled things out of the fire, but this time there was no saving grace. I was a failure. I walked toward Sattes and eventually saw the old Sattes Elementary School. Walking past the school, I continued on toward downtown Nitro, walking along the bypass.

I finally reached Second Avenue and I walked past 8th Street toward 21st Street. At the head of 8th street is where my mom and dad lived when they were first married. Years later, in this same house, I would enjoy Christmas with my aunt and uncle with bubble lights on their tree.

I could hardly stand it when my aunt would go googly eyed over Liberace. Oh my goodness, I couldn't stand him as a little boy and disliked his music. But she had bubble lights, and we didn't. So my brother, cousin and I would sit in the living room and watch the lights bubble even when Liberace was on television.

Past 8th Street, I sauntered up the sidewalk past 12th street. On this street, near Main Avenue, my dad was born. Ahead was 16th street where I moved to a second-floor apartment as a little boy. It was in this apartment where the floor stomping episode occurred in our hallway. Not far from this spot was the home of a girl I liked in junior high school. She was one of the few who moved on after high school and I didn't see again for decades.

Nearby, on 2nd Avenue, the old Church of God was built with the help of my grandfather and my dad. My grandfather was always a Church of God member until his later life when he joined the Independent Methodist Church. It was out on Old Dixie Highway, outside of Springfield, Georgia. My grandfather was well liked, and when he passed away, he was buried in the little cemetery across the road from the church. This was the cemetery that my son landscaped for his Eagle Scout project in the early 1990s.

Pop, my grandfather, was buried in the old traditional southern manner in Georgia. Instead of everyone walking away from the graveside after the graveside service, the workmen began filling the grave immediately. This surprised my dad and my brother. Later, after the burial, Dad said that perhaps that was a better send off than walking away leaving him unburied. It brought finality to the ceremony.

Finally I arrived at 21st Street and walked that last mile and half with tears, not really feeling sorry for myself, but mad at myself for throwing away my tuition and my year of college. When I arrived at home, I was sick. I had to explain to my mom what happened, and she was on my case for my laziness. Alas, I was so upset that I became violently ill and threw up in the front yard. I was really sick to my stomach and feeling very ill when the worst thing could have happened. Up the driveway, drove my old friend, Hannah, from Virginia with her parents. Hannah was attending a school in North Carolina. She was a year older than I was, and she was in her junior year. She made good grades. What was I going to say? How could I explain that I was sick, and the last thing I needed was some girl asking a lot of questions? My mom, seeing the terror on my face, told me to relax and clean up for dinner. After dinner, we sat in the living room and talked about growing up in Virginia and all our adventures as friends. The stories were funny and helped me get over my traumatic day.

Chapter 3

EXPERIENCE WITH A RECRUITER– JOHNSON'S WAR–JANUARY 1968

A few days after walking home from college, I went job hunting. I found work at Vimasco Paint Corporation starting in the fall of 1967. I worked for a quiet, blonde-haired man named Thomas. Thomas and I got along well, and I learned the lab work quickly, checking viscosity of paint and fire retardant coverings, and the grade of silicone samples sent to the lab. Each shipment was tested for clarity and cleanliness.

During lunch, Tom and I would set up a large-mouth jar along the back wall. We baited the jar with some peanut butter and jelly bread. A long string was thrown over the rafter and tied to the mouth of the jar. Eventually, an unsuspecting mouse would wander into the jar and with a quick pull was captured. We had plenty of test paint available so we put a dab of paint on the mouse's back and let him go back to his environs. Sometimes we would capture the same mouse, but more often not. It was a good lesson in statistical analysis Thomas explained to me.

Handling the mice reminded me of the rats I kept while I was in the twelfth grade. Every day I fed them and sometimes cleaned a cage while they clung on to me like orphaned squirrels. I used heavy gloves to handle them, but they were quite gentle.

In early December 1967, three things happened that I will never forget. First, the moth man was sighted flying all over Point Pleasant, West Virginia. Secondly, the Silver Bridge fell into the Ohio River, killing dozens of people. This bridge spanned the river between Point Pleasant and Gallipolis, Ohio. Third, I received my first notice for a draft physical, which I passed at Beckley, West Virginia. You only received two physicals before your draft notice was sent to your home. I decided to wait until I had my second physical to join the military.

Eventually, my second notice for a physical came out about one month later. I was about to be drafted, and I had a decision to make. I always wanted to serve in the US Army. I wasn't disturbed by a three-year commitment or the additional three years of inactive reserve. I thought about Special Forces, but you had to be a sergeant and know how to speak a foreign language — and usually these men were much older than a nine-teen-year-old boy.

I went to Charleston in early January to see a recruiter after my first physical. My draft status changed from II-S to I-A. This meant that I was going to be drafted. In 1968, you didn't wait on a lottery; there was no lottery. You were automat-ically drafted if you were not attending college. Just about every young man I knew was going into the service in 1967, '68, and '69.

I arrived at the courthouse on 500 Quarrier Street, in Charleston, West Virginia. At first I tried the Air Force. Walking up to the door, the Air Force recruiter was standing in the door, blocking it and talking with another recruiter. He looked at me and said, "What do you need?" I mentioned I had an interest in the Air Force and I asked whether he could he tell me what fields might be avail-able in the Air Force. He looked at me and said, "It's not what does the Air Force have for you, boy, but what have you got to give to the Air Force?" I answered with a sarcastic, "Not a thing!" My temper got the best of me, and I went next door to speak with the Army.

The recruiter heaped a battery of tests on me before lunch, and after lunch I came back to see what was available. The Army recruiter gave me a very thick book and said, "Pick any MOS (Military Occupation Specialty) in this book; you qualified for all the MOS positions the Army offers." So, I took the book and sat down and began thumbing through hundreds of MOS duties. Hoping there might be something in forestry, I asked a simple question, "Do you have anything in here that might pertain to forestry-type duties?" It was a simple question asked by a nineteen-year-old boy. "Look, son, this is the Army; we don't have any forestry jobs. Keep looking" was his answer. So, I kept looking.

"Hmmmm, here's an interesting job, 'asphalt tester for the Army Engineers."

"No, no, no, that's just a fancy word for infantry. The Army calls them crunchies; that's the noise made when tanks run over their helmets in combat, making a crunching sound. Keep looking," the recruiter snorted, so I kept looking.

"How about X-ray technician, or medical technician?"

"I'll check." The Army recruiter made a quick phone call. "No, it's filled up; no medical MOSs are open at this time. Pick another one," he patiently quipped.

I continued to thumb through hundreds of jobs. Finally I spied an interesting job, "How about 96B20 combat order of battle intelligence analyst? This looks pretty interesting, keeping track of enemy units and all. It looks like something I'd find interesting."

He made a phone call, "Yes, I can get you into school, and, I can cut you a contract guaranteeing you the school will have a slot for you. How about it?"

I thought for a moment. He chimed in, "It comes with an automatic promotion to Private E-2. How about it?"

"Sure, I think I'd like that type of job," I said. So, I signed up for three years as a 96B20, not realizing that it was my one-way ticket to Vietnam, the only place the US Army had a real need of a combat order of battle analyst.

When I got home and bragged about joining the US Army, my dad was furious. He grabbed a *Charleston Daily Mail* newspaper. On the front page was an article about a US Marine squad ambushed in South Vietnam. They were summarily executed and mutilated. Dad threw the paper at me and said, "There! There is what war is all about. There's your damn army; it's nothing but death and destruction." I don't think he meant it that way, but he was scared. His oldest boy had just joined the US Army at a time when the war was heating up and men were dying by the dozens every single day. Dad never threw it in my face after that. As a matter of fact, he was very proud of me from the day I left for basic training to the day he died. I reported to Beckley in January for my final physical and induction. It was 20 January 1968.

A draft notice was sent to my home dated 22 January 1968. Fortunately, I had already joined the US Army on the twenty-second. When I called home, Mom was crying and sobbing. "They've drafted you!" she sobbed.

"Mom, Mom, listen, I've already joined. I'm on my way to Fort Knox; I'm already in the US Army!"

"What do I do with this letter?" she replied.

"Throw it away!" I said.

She didn't throw it away, and I still have my draft induction notice dated 22 January 1968 for an induction of 13 February 1968 at 8:30 a.m. My induction notice started out by saying; "Greeting," not Greetings. Regardless of what it said, I was now a volunteer for the Regular Army, and on my way to Fort Knox, Kentucky.

I joined the United States Army on 22 January 1968 at Beckley, West Virginia. On the day I joined the US Army, every fifth man that was drafted was asked to step forward, and they became a US Marine. So much for volunteering; in January 1968 this was the Marines' way of getting a few good men. In those days, there were very few women in the services. I did not see a female soldier until I became an instructor at the United States Army Intelligence School in March of 1970. In those days you were assigned a serial number. My US Army Serial Number began with the prefix "RA" for Regular Army.

The bus left Beckley, West Virginia, for Louisville, Kentucky. It was mid-morning when we climbed aboard. I was carrying a small bag with several changes of T-shirts, and another dress shirt, folded and rolled, socks, and toiletry kit. The ride toward Huntington was familiar, but soon we crossed over into eastern Kentucky, and this terrain was different and interesting. I remember going through, or near, Bowling Green. The hills were undulating, and the mountains and woods gave way for large, bright green pastures. I thought of horses and how pleasant this country looked.

As dusk fell, we were nearing Louisville, Kentucky, and the beginning of my military career. The bus weaved its way to the terminal and parked. We eased off the bus and into the terminal. A sergeant met us and guided us to a pickup point. He took roll call and kept us in one tight area inside the terminal. Finally a military-style bus pulled up, similar to a school bus with terribly padded seats and stuffy. We were crowded onto the bus, military style, from the back to the front. After sitting down, I tried to find my trip to Fort Knox interesting. I watched the dark hills roll by, with an occasional business here and there. I couldn't make out any features. The terrain matched my mood, dark and featureless. I was going into the US Army, and nothing could stop this adventure.

Chapter 4

GET OFF MY BUS!—23 JANUARY 1968

We approached Fort Knox and stopped at the gate for a brief moment before the "wave" of a military policeman's hand sent us in. As the bus stopped in front of a large administration building, a large sergeant, followed by two other sergeants, boomed out, "Who is the toughest man on this bus?" Of course there is always that one person that is going to raise his hand. All three Sergeants sprung like leopards and grabbed the man by his collar and jacket, and drug him off the bus, where they commenced to beat him about the face and shoulders. After knocking him down several times and pulling him back up, the big sergeant came back on board. "Any more tough guys on here?" You could have heard a pin drop. "Then GET OFF MY BUS!" he yelled, and everyone scrambled to get off the bus and line up on the little footprints in front of the Admin building.

Fort Knox is a beautiful fort, nestled in the foothills along the Ohio River near Louisville Kentucky. I stayed in the same barracks area and trained in the same training area and parade fields you see in the movie *Stripes*. As a matter of fact, we had the same characters in basic training, the fat guy, the killer, and the wise cracker. I sometimes wonder if the guy that wrote the script for the movie *Stripes* went through basic training with me.

I was assigned to Delta Company, 18th Training Battalion, 5th Training Brigade. As far as I can figure out, Fort Knox had the 3rd, 4th, and 5th Training Brigades. Delta Company's motto was "We're the best; to hell with the rest, Delta 18−5." We'd yell that out, and then we would sit down. The 2nd Platoon, Delta Company, had fifty-five men assigned to it. It was considered an RA (regular army) platoon; meaning most of us were volunteers. Of the fifty-five men, seven were black, no Hispanics, and the rest white. Five of the troopers were from West Virginia, and the rest were from Ohio, Kentucky, and Michigan. We had at least one guy who was a gang murderer, and one guy who called himself Jesus Christ. "Jesus" was eventually given a blanket party, thrown down the steps at least three times, and he escaped with his life by running out the door half naked. We threw his wall locker and all his belongings out into the yard between barracks. He never came back to our company, and we never got into trouble. That is the way we handled troublemakers in the '60s.

My platoon sergeants were Sergeant Holly, Corporal Merrit, and Sergeant First Class McBride. Holly was a Vietnam veteran, Merrit was a loser of a corporal, and Sergeant McBride was a World War II veteran. McBride was a quiet black man who only yelled at us once in eight weeks of training. And, it wasn't a yell; it was more of a statement. We had spent the morning practicing the manual of arms, that is, right shoulder and left shoulder arms, and so on. We kept screwing this up. Finally, he stopped everyone in their tracks and made us stand at attention. Pacing back and forth in front of us, he finally looked at us and said in a very quiet manner, "When they drafted you idiots, they were scrapping the bottom of the barrel." That's about all the yelling we got out of him. However, he was dead serious, so we continued training until he was satisfied.

Sergeant Holly, a Vietnam combat veteran, was a different story. He wanted to make sure he had men, not women, in his company. He was very demeaning, intimidating, and at times mean spirited. On one occasion in the chow hall, Sergeant Holly put on a pair of boxing gloves and made those that were caught talking to stand up and lean against a partitioned wall. After they put their nose against the wall, he walked around on the other side and began punching the partition. No bloody noses, but we all learned to keep quiet while eating or our face would bounce off the partition.

Corporal Merrit, on the other hand, was just a drunk and crazy soldier. He would spend hours throwing his bread knife at pictures of women pinned on the back of a door in the upstairs NCO (Non Commissioned Officer) room. You would hear a "swoosh" then "thud and brrrrriinnnng" as the knife would shudder to a final stop. He was dangerous when he was drunk. He was not a good NCO. One night he came into the barracks at about 3:00 a.m. and made us gather all our boots and go upstairs and throw them into the street below. Everyone had two pair of boots, one pair we painted a "white dot" on the upper back of the boot. The pair without the dot were called "black dot" boots. All fifty-five platoon members scrambled upstairs with two pair of boots and threw them out into the street. Inside each pair of boots we had written our name, rank, and serial number. I suppose this exercise was to find out who among us did not do as we were told. After an hour of scrambling outside, all boots were returned, whereupon I had two pair of boots to spit shine and shine the soles, too.

Such was the life of a young nineteen-year-old soldier. It was much tougher than today's basic training, but I think every old soldier has said the same thing. In those days they stomped on your feet if you were out of step or kicked you in the shinbone to make sure you knew left from right. They could smack you, punch you, and hit you with their helmets if you were acting up. They also carried small hickory sticks to motivate you on the obstacle course. Moving too slowly? You got a whack on the butt! And, of course, if you stood up to them, you would get a good beating.

I learned to pay attention and do what I was told to do without question. Once I remember duck walking around a ten-acre field, quacking like a duck. If you didn't duck walk fast enough, the drill instructors (DIs) would whack you with their stick. I think the term used is, "You're really smart or really strong in the Army."

I learned to fire the M-14 rifle. The M-14 weighs 8.6 pounds and has a very long-barrel and is a well-built rifle. I shot expert, hitting sixty-seven out of eighty pop-up targets, including all pop-up targets at 500 yards. My biggest problem with pop-up targets were the ten and twenty yard targets — the close ones. The M-14 did not lend itself to close-in targets. I usually shot over their heads. This was a problem I hoped the M-16 would solve.

I learned the US Army's method of "quick kill." We started shooting at small spinning targets with BB guns and eventually shot at metal disks tossed into the air. When you could hit those discs regularly, you shot at a quarter. Hit the quarter, and you shot at a dime. Hit the dime tossed in the air, and you graduated to the quick kill night-firing course.

At night we would shoot at targets without actually aiming, shooting from the hip and the shoulder with both eyes open. The lights would shine bright for several seconds, and then there was complete darkness, and you fired at what you thought was your target. Lights came back on, and you went down range to see if you hit what you thought you were shooting at.

Quick kill training probably saved a lot of lives in Vietnam; the reaction time of GI meeting VC in face-to-face combat meant the person who reacted quickest lived to talk about it. Additionally, we were taught bayonet training. I learned to parry and thrust, using the short- and long-thrust methods. With a bayonet attached the M-14 was an excellent weapon for hand-to-hand combat.

I learned numerous first aid tricks, like how to stop a sucking chest wound with a pack of cigarettes. I learned other useful combat skills like fire and maneuver, and how to cross obstacles like a log or a fence or tangle foot, a triangular-shaped barbed wire fence, under fire. In addition, we spent time at night using a touch-and-feel method for finding fences and booby trap trip wires with our hands. The training was challenging, but I did very well. My body grew from a 5 feet, 9 inch, 128-pound skinny kid to a 6 feet, 156-pound man in eight weeks!

There were two housing areas for basic training in 1968. Disney Land was a modern barracks, made of brick, and laid out in a more modern format. We often envied those housed in Disney Land and would march by their barracks and marvel at how warm and inviting they looked compared to our World War II wooden barracks. Our two-story barracks were made of wood, drafty, and heated by a coal fired furnace.

The barracks housed the platoon sergeant and assistant and forty-eight recruits, twenty-four downstairs and twenty-four upstairs. Each barracks was divided into squads with an acting squad leader. The building only had one latrine facility, with urinals and flushing toilets, but no partitions between toilets. Only one long skinny room was used as the shower stall. Everyone took a shower next to each other; there was no privacy anywhere in a barracks.

Mail call was announced once a day, in the evening after training. In between shining boots and cleaning gear, you would write a letter to your parents or a girlfriend. I also wrote a few more letters to my grandparents and my aunts, but for the most part, lights out came early. Everyone was so tired; most of us went to sleep around 9:00 p.m., or 2100 hours.

The chow hall was a nice break, but standing in line at parade rest, arm's length apart, was not fun. Even worse was the required quick crawl through the sand pit on your stomach and doing the hand rails, then running to the chow line. If you fell off the hand-over-hand rails, you got to do the whole thing over again. Inside the chow hall, you were given approximately 3,000 to 4,000 calories per serving, lots of mashed potatoes, SOS (chipped beef on biscuits and gravy) or some other high-calorie food. It was pretty bland, and I heard they used "saltpeter" in the food to dissuade sexual feelings. It probably worked as most of us were too tired to act that way in the latrine.

Meals were very fast, and cleanup was completed in record time. We went back out the door to the barracks, but the latrines were off limits. It is here that I made my biggest mistake at Fort Knox; I had to go! Sitting alone in the latrine, I thought I could finish and get back into the bay without getting caught. I was not fast enough. The DI allowed me to finish, and then I caught his full wrath. I was assigned additional duty on Saturday afternoon, my only real time off to write letters and I was cleaning a galvanized aluminum garbage can with a can of "Brasso." This pointless cleaning duty produced a very clean garbage can. It took me several hours to complete and ruined my time to write letters home.

Barracks life was a strain on everyone, although we adjusted, individualism melted away. My bunk buddy was a very large young man from Detroit. He was given the choice of prison or the military by a judge for second-degree manslaughter. He had killed a boy messing with his girlfriend. That is all I knew about his home life; I didn't pry too much. He was very large, on the fat side, and when we ran down misery and up heartbreak, he needed help. We would take turns carrying his rifle and sometimes his pack. Others would grab his belt and make him run. We did not want him to fall down because we would be made to stop and march back and forth over his body on the ground until he decided to pull himself up. It was very humiliating and degrading. None of us wanted that to happen to our big man. Later on in basic, I would help him through the machine gun training pit.

A good friend of mine from Louisville set up a date for me on a free weekend that I earned for shooting expert on the rifle range. Darlene accompanied Roy's girlfriend and his mother to Fort Knox to visit us. I had a chance to sit beside a very pretty girl and take them on a tour of our training areas. Finally, we stopped in the parking lot outside our barracks. It was cold outside, but we were bundled up in the back seat. Darlene allowed me to kiss her, and for a little while I was in another world. Roy's mother was not watching us, but she knew we were kissing in the back seat. To be honest, this was truly the break I needed during basic training. Darlene was a great kisser and a sweet girl. She took off her St. Christopher medal, which hung from a fine chain, and put it around my neck. She asked me to promise her I would be safe. I said I would, and she kissed me again. I wore that medal through all eighteen months of duty in Vietnam.

In the last weeks of basic training, our platoon marched out to the field for a week-long road march and final test prior to graduation. It was typical US Army weather. We started on the road march on a crisp February morning. It was cold, and frost covered the ground. As the day matured, the weather warmed, and before lunchtime we wanted to strip off our heavy field jackets. Marching some ten miles or so, we stopped for lunch in a wooded area. Here we ate standing up at makeshift picnic tables made out of tarmac material. It was raining at that point, and that added to our misery. The meal was gravy on biscuits. The army calls it SOS, and that is not an endearing term. To this very day I cannot stand eating SOS, and I avoid it at all costs.

After lunch, we proceeded to march into a hilly area where eventually the platoon snaked its way down into a ravine. We stopped and prepared fighting positions in readying to ford a small river. One by one, single file, each man filtered across the river to the other side, whereupon we immediately pulled off our boots and put on dry socks. We put the wet socks under our fatigue shirts, next to our body, to dry out from body heat and continued our march.

The sun set as we hit mile 20, and the column was in combat formation along a small paved road. A combat formation is a single-file column on each side of the road. Each man was several feet apart. This spread us out over a long area along the highway. No one was talking; the column, solemn and quiet. We pushed ahead another six miles that night, stopping somewhere in central Kentucky at a ravine, surrounded by woods. In this area, probably ten acres in size, each platoon member was issued a small tent half. We buddied up to make a full tent and pitched our tent. Darn, I thought, that's a good-looking tent. It wasn't sagging or droopy, but looked very professional. It was tight and stood erect, and the front and back guide wires were perfect.

We crawled into our tent, rifle inside the sleeping bag with you, and tried to sleep. Sometime that night, one of our platoon members got up to go to the bathroom. He tripped over our guide wire, snapping the front tent pole in half. *Dang*, I thought, *now what*? We took a pair of socks and repaired the tent pole so that it stood erect and held the pressure of the tent. It was Yankee inge-nuity at its best, and we put our tent back up.

The next day we took turns shaving in cold water poured into our helmet shell. The old steel pots were good for shaving out of, digging fox holes, or killing an enemy in hand-to-hand combat. The weather changed yet again to cold with clouds rolling in.

We saddled up and prepared to march again to the maneuver rifle ranges. It began to snow. The day before we were burning up from heat and were drenched by rain; today we were going to freeze in a white wintry blizzard! When we reached the rifle ranges, the snow partially cov-ered the ground, the wind was crisp, and everyone was dressed in large overcoats, or field coats, that were issued at the range. The field coats, with our "pile" caps, gave us the impression that we were in the Russian army.

At the maneuver ranges we practiced fire and maneuver on a live fire range, moving in alpha and bravo fire team formations. We moved past live fire on the range to toss a grenade into an open window or jump over a wall or crawl up over a log. As you moved down this obstacle course, your buddies were shooting past you on either side. Once you took position to fire at pop-up targets, your buddies moved past you in their firing lanes. We hopscotched across this open course and completed it in a snowstorm. After this training the snow stopped and it began to clear. We traded in our field coats for our field jackets.

After a day on the fire-and-maneuver range, we hiked down to a set of athletic seats. Here we received our briefing on the live-fire range and we were instructed how to cross over the open terrain with a 7.62mm machine gun (M-60) firing over our heads. This is what every young boy fears about basic training, the dreaded live-fire range. I had heard horror stories of young men who panicked and stood up during the exercise and were immediately cut down in a hail of machine gun bullets.

These stories always ran rampant in the ranks. I honestly think the DI's planted these tales in order to make sure you kept your head down. The range was laid out with large round pits that held explosives. It was said those pits were armed with about a half stick of dynamite.

At the beginning of the range, a cat walk that was below ground level allowed each platoon to enter into the pit at one time. Fifty men would snake their way along the catwalk, hugging the wall. On command of a whistle, the men would reach their rifles over the parapet and climb up, each man carefully keeping his butt and shoulders as low as possible. Bullets would buzz overhead, sounding like hornets on fire. You would crawl about fifteen feet and then cross over a telephone pole–like log lying on the ground. The rifle went over first, then body. Next would be three strands of tangle foot. Meanwhile explosions would cook off and raise you off the ground. The concussion would reverberate through your body, making your insides dance.

I remember the ground was wet from snow and rain falling during the day. The explosions would throw mud and sand all over you. You learned to protect your rifle at all costs, and keeping it dry and clean as possible was something you paid attention to.

When you hit a barb wire fence called "tangle foot", you had to roll over on your back, laying your M-14 rifle on your stomach with the lever down, so the wire wouldn't get caught on it. Everyone was instructed to use the rifle to let the wire slide down the rifle and as you pushed yourself forward. The reason why you were taught this maneuver is because tangle foot was usually about six inches off the ground. It was here, under the tangle foot wire, that the biggest man in our platoon, the murderer, my bunk mate, used my head as a springboard to get through the tangle-foot wire. Eventually, I pushed him through, and we finally reached the safety area where we could stand up and go forward. This was a milestone in my military career, and I was glad it was over. After this, I figured I could do most anything.

All of our physical fitness was taken in fatigues and combat boots. There were no tennis shoes and running clothes allowed. We did the mile run, the hand-bars, rope climb, and other obstacles, all while wearing our combat boots. In my mind, physical fitness was tougher in 1968. I would guess World War II vets said that about us. But

I would bet our training was not that much different than World War II, a war that ended a scant twenty-three years before 1968.

Sundays were the best days in basic training. Before lunch, we would all dress in our OG 44s, a heavy wool fatigue uniform and put on spit-shined boots and our helmet liners, and we were allowed to walk to the church of our choice. There were several. The one I enjoyed visiting was the same church I guarded on patrol on Sundays when I had guard duty. The OG 44 was a warm and sharp-looking uniform. The US Army gave up a really good-looking uniform when they did away with the OG 44. Those also were holdover uniforms from World War II.

The day I graduated from basic training, rioters in Baltimore, Maryland, were burning down the city. None of us were aware of this; we did not receive news of the Tet Offensive or what was going on in the nation. We were too busy surviving basic.

Upon graduation we were bussed from Fort Knox to waiting aircraft. It was my first ride on a jet airliner, and I was both excited and apprehensive. I remember sitting down, waiting to taxi to the runway and our initial takeoff. I was truly surprised at the power of the jet engines and how much faster we reached high speed. My last airplane ride had been on an old DC-3 in the early 1950s.

We arrived at Freedom Field in Baltimore late at night on board a jet aircraft. We were bused to the intelligence school, located in Dundalk, Baltimore. The city was in turmoil and chaos. Whole blocks of Baltimore were on fire, businesses and homes and whatever else near the fire was consumed. The rioting continued for several days, even threatening the base.

The next day, I spent several hours looking for a bomb in the intelligence barracks area. We opened every wall locker and foot locker and inspected every nook and cranny. No bomb was found. That night I was given guard duty to walk the perimeter of the fence at Fort Holabird, looking for intruders or any mischief outside or near our fence line. Eventually, the riots died down, and we were allowed some leave time to go home. It was the first time I was able to catch a cab to Freedom Field and fly to Charleston, West Virginia.

Chapter 5

INTELLIGENCE SCHOOL–MARCH TO AUGUST 1968

Intelligence school was nine weeks long. I caught on how to analyze enemy prisoner-of-war reports and captured documents, and how to write Synchronized Predeployment and Operational Tracker (SPOT) Intelligence Reports. I mastered the study of enemy forces and their order of battle, and how a fighting unit is organized, trains, and conducts combat operations. I felt good taking these classes and understood every facet of intelligence.

The classes at Fort Holabird ranged from an in-depth study of maps, photographs, and order-of-battle reports to special-agent reports (SPAR) and side-looking radar (SLAR) reports. We became adept at understanding lines of communication, such as highways, waterways, railways, and logistics depots. We studied cultural aspects, such as political boundaries, urban areas, telecommunications, and ethnic and tribal groups. Intelligence studies looked at engineering aspects of terrain, including soils, geology materials, weather and climate, and bomb damage assessment (BDA). Intelligence classes even covered defoliation and photo missions. It was quite in-depth to say the least!

I found the most interesting subject, albeit possibly the most dry, was the organization of combat units. We studied several theories, including the triangle theory and the rectangle theory. The triangle concept was classic Soviet Union armed forces structure. Soviet armed forces were usually built on three units at every level of the same type, augmented by a fourth support unit. Soviet infantry divisions usually had three infantry regiments supported by a tank regiment. These regiments were made up of three combat battalions and a combat support battalion. Of course, they also had other support units such as artillery, signals, medical, and so forth.

The battalion becomes the "building block" of almost every combat force in the world. It comes from Napoleon whose theory of the battalion was the largest unit in the field one man could command. The commander can see every man on the field of combat under his command. That was his concept.

A classic example of a "battalion" operating in combat is the movie *We Were Soldiers.* The movie starring Mel Gibson as Lieutenant General (then Lieutenant Colonel) Hal Moore as commander of the 1st Battalion, 7th Cavalry Regiment, 1st Cavalry Division. (1st Cav was still organized on the regimental system). It shows an outstanding concept of how one man commands and controls a combat battalion in a hostile situation (Movie *We Were Soldiers*, Drama 2010).

The rectangle theory was classic US doctrine, right out of 1960s. The rectangle hypothesis was basically the new US Army, Reorganization Of Army Divisions (ROAD). Each division was made up of infantry brigades, supported by a heavy-weapons brigade or battalion. Additional support battalions, such as an aviation battalion, or a self-propelled howitzer battalion, made up the brigade.

The biggest difference between the Russian regimental system and the US Army brigade system is the size of the headquarters support element. A larger support staff allows for supporting additional units in combat. A brigade can be made up of many combat and support battalions without changing much of its unit support capability. This is why a US Army brigade may be comparable to the size of a Russian division. The Cuban armed forces were the only communist forces that adopted US doctrine in those days; all other communist countries used the Russian triangle theory.

The study of how all forces of the world are designed for combat, to include naval and air forces, is a fascinating subject. Ever changing, evolving, and allowing new technology, the combat forces evolve over the years. For instance in 1918, a US Army division had about 18,000 riflemen. The infantry division back then probably covered less than a mile in width and a mile in depth, compared to today's infantry division around 11,000 men (plus or minus). Its front can be many more miles wide with fewer men, and its depth is many times deeper than that of a unit in World War I. Thus, much fewer men cover more area in combat. This is due to the lethality of today's weapons and technology used on the battlefield.

My primary instructors were Lt. Chasen, (I can't recall his face); SSgt. O'Leary, a dark-haired fellow from up north somewhere, and Sgt. Forest, a young E5 "hard stripe" Marine sergeant who had just returned from Vietnam. We stayed in the large barracks building that spanned the parade field where a huge garrison flag flew. Early mornings, we awakened to reveille, and we had just minutes to dress in the uniform of the day and rush to formation. At formation, about five hundred of us were lined up by platoons. Our platoon leader was a Marine. The Marines used the same school for their combat order of battle analysts and other intelligence specialists. We were marched to chow and stood at parade rest until we received our meal.

We were assigned KP (Kitchen Police) duty regularly. I worked in the chow hall, peeling potatoes. I also helped cook green beans and eggs and sausage and fixed the lunch meal. It was an all-day affair, working in the mess hall. After the evening meal, we cleaned that kitchen up spic and span. I learned how to twirl a mop to pick up water or a spilled drink. I loved pots and pans. They were dirty, but I didn't care; that was a challenge and I enjoyed that job.

While working in the mess hall, I told my buddies one of my stories. "Back when I was a kid, probably in the mid '60s, we built a cabin, you know, a fort." They listened intently as we clanged pots and silverware, getting it clean. "That old fort had railroad 2 × 4s made out of red oak. You couldn't drive a nail through that stuff if your life depended on it." I leaned sideways to show them how it was about to fall over. "Unfortunately, that stupid fort began to lean worse. By the time we finished, it was six feet tall, but leaning toward Fishers." Someone asked me where was Fishers? I had no clue, so I said, "It's somewhere down-stream." I paused. "We wanted to camp out that night, so a friend and his cousin, Boo, Dave, and I camped out in that little fort."

I continued, "We had flashlights and candy and cookies. Fig Newtons. Well, Mom and Dad wanted to find out how the camping trip was going. They slipped outside and sat on the back porch and listened. You know little boys hardly can be still. Then Barry's cousin, Roger, had to go to the bathroom. 'Where can I go?' he whined. I said, 'Go outside where it's dark and go. There is nobody up, whose gonna see you?' So outside he went, and he found him a spot. He wet against the fort, and my brother screamed, 'He's peed on the Fig Newtons' as it splashed through the walls onto the cookies! My mom and dad almost had heart attacks from laughing so hard. They went inside and continued to laugh and giggle and laugh again for an hour or so. Needless to say, we lost our treasured cookies, soiled by Roger."

Well, that got a chuckle and a laugh out of everyone and helped push us through the drudgery of KP duty. The story reminded me of another fort we tried to build up behind Mr. Ghia's barn. "Our fort was going to be built on top of a rock cliff. It gave us good protection because the only way up to the fort was to climb up by rope.

Barry was with us, and the three of us were going to build a fort that overlooked the holler behind Mr. Ghia's house and barn. All day we had hauled 2 × 4 pine boards and plywood up the face of a two-story cliff. It was a steep fall, and there was no other way up unless you went a football-field length to find a shelf, or a safer way up the cliff without a rope. That was too far to drag stuff to the top, so we figured the rope was the quickest way up.

Everything was going just fine until Dave was tasked to bring up the nails we kept in a mason jar. David grabbed the rope and was actually climbing one-handed, holding the jar of nails in the other, juggling it with his chin, and pressing the jar against his body. About halfway up the rock face, he yelled up to me, "Here, Kenny, take these." He tossed that mason jar up toward me. The jar fell short, and I reached for it but missed. When the jar hit the face of the rock cliff it broke into a million pieces! Glass and nails rained down on David, hitting him in the face and body, and he let go of the rope and fell probably fifteen feet to the base of the cliff. We watched in horror as he hit square in the middle of the biggest briar patch up the holler, maybe in all of Morgan's Creek. There were so many briars and stickers that they cushioned his fall, and he fell like a feather into a sea of stickers.

Immediately we climbed down the rope, but we couldn't help him because of the thickness of the briar patch. Barry and I hunted for sticks that were about five feet long. We began to beat the briars, breaking them down and pushing a pathway to Dave who was fine, just stuck. We helped unhook him and wrestled our way out of the briars to safety. We decided that that fort would have to become just a campground. We lost our nails, and it was just too hard to continue, so we abandoned the fort." The stories were fun to tell, and actually I was able to make many friends because I was full of it. I always had a comeback or a story, and that kept conversation lively.

I was afraid of school because I felt I was a poor student and would flunk out of intelligence school. Some people call the school an oxymoron, but truly it was a pretty intense training course. The time came to start classes, and I would have to find a way to study. Classes covered map reading, mosaic photographs, the study of Army, Navy, and Air Force order of battle for the Soviet Union and China, our two biggest adversaries, and of course, the North Vietnamese Army (NVA) and Viet Cong (VC) order of battle in Vietnam. Some of my Army Security Agency (ASA) buddies wrote some good articles on "Military Intelligence is not an Oxymoron." I think readers should research ASA in Vietnam and learn how complex and how very good we were at supporting ground troops with intelligence.

We had cross pollination of other classes, such as imagery interpretation, prisoner-of-war inter-rogation, and counterintelligence operations. I soon settled into my home at Fort Holabird and began good study habits. The tests and quizzes were tough and demanding. They didn't give you any leeway on passing tests. You either knew the material, or you failed that test.

Fort Holabird was on about forty acres of land. It was enclosed inside a single eight-foot-high fence and had two main entrances — the entrance off of Holabird Avenue and an entrance off of Dundalk Avenue. Nestled between the huge General Motors plant and Dundalk Avenue, Fort Holabird was the home of all the major US Army intelligence military occupational specialties (MOS). US Army counterintelligence students were mixed with imagery interpreters, prisoner-of-war interrogators, and intelligence analysts. All students lived in the large barracks and marched to and from school every day. Along Holabird Avenue were long gray barracks with no windows. I was told they were World War II prison buildings for German prisoners.

I was talking with my father-in-law and found out he was assigned to Fort Holabird in 1922. He was in transportation and drove trucks in a transportation company. Fort Holabird was a transportation training school in 1922. In the middle of the campus, there is a very large hill that looks out of place and has a road going up one side and down the other. This iconic hill was out of place, as Fort

Holabird was flat as a fritter. My father-in-law said he remembered driving over that structure many times in different vehicles for training (Mr. Harry Bardell; 1971).

During the school we were visited by Army Intelligence Officer Major Nick Rowe. He gave us an outstanding briefing on his harrowing captivity with the Viet Cong and his escape. He was captured in 1963, and his story is one of courage and honor. For five years, they beat him, tortured him, and questioned him over and over about intelligence information he may have about the Special Forces in South Vietnam. Over and over, he refused to tell them anything, even after they showed him evidence that someone in America had taken pictures of his home and wife and family. This information was used during his brutal interrogations. This convinced him that there were inside spies at work in the United States, who were probably antiwar Americans. Nick was earmarked for execution. He was being led to the place of execution when he jumped his captors and escaped.

I was able to speak to Colonel Rowe at an Air National Guard Conference in Charlotte North Carolina many years later. He was a very intelligent and humble officer. I admired him, and it was truly a pleasure to sit and talk about his experiences in Vietnam.

Later in 1989, Colonel Rowe was gunned down in the Philippines by the Communist New People's Army. These cowards shot him at close range; he never had a chance. On that day, the US Army lost a true national hero. I hope all who read my book will seek out his book, *Five Years to Freedom*, and read his memoirs of his five-year captivity and daring escape.

The intelligence course was straightforward. I started school in May of 1968 and completed the nine-week course on 10 July 1968. There were five "2-hour" exams worth 100 points each, two practical exams, and eight quizzes, ten points each, to make a grand total of 600 points. You needed 413 points to pass. Out of sixty-two persons in the class, I came in as thirty-sixth in the class. My score was 478 points out of 600. I passed and was promoted to specialist 4th class on 10 July 1968. I waited for orders from Higher HQ.

The same Quonset huts where I attended intelligence school are still there today. They are the file depositories for the Defense Investigation Service. You can see them from Dundalk Boulevard in

Baltimore, Maryland. That is about all that's left of Fort Holabird.

Graduation Day was approaching, and on 16 July 1968, I graduated from the US Army Intelligence School, Department of Combat Intelligence, Combat Order of Battle School. Now, this was pretty impressive, considering a year earlier I was considered a complete idiot in college. Regardless, I was graduating in the middle of our class, and my mom and dad and two brothers were coming for my graduation.

Something odd happened when my dad arrived at Fort Holabird housing and was greeted with much aplomb. He was called Sir, and was given the "top VIP room" at housing. I wondered what on earth was going on. One of the senior sergeants asked me how long had my dad been in the military. Well, to be honest, I told him, my dad was 4F during World War II. He contemplated suicide because it was such a stigma, a very dishonorable thing to be left behind. No, he was never in the military. The sergeant shook his head and grinned at me, "Luikart, those idiots up there at housing think he's a general." I was shocked.

I stammered, "Well, what should I do?"

"Nothing," he replied. "Let him be a general for one day then go home having been given the best room on base." He laughed hard and shook his head and left. He told everyone that my dad was General Luikart. I was so embarrassed and afraid someone higher up would find out. But in the end, it worked out as I was released to go with my parents right after graduation. Rank has its privileges.

Well, Dad was a general for a day, and he didn't know it. They gave him a good seat at graduation, and he was greeted by some of the brass on base. He just took it in stride and had a good time. I was so grateful they came to pick me up and took me to Virginia on vacation with them. I needed a break between Holabird, Maryland, and Oakland, California.

Chapter 6

SPECIAL ORDER NO. 148–16 JULY 1968 TO AUGUST 1968

I mmediately after graduation from US Army Intelligence School (USAINTS), I was given about three weeks leave between completing school and reporting to Oakland, California, for my flight to Vietnam on August 10. Special Order Number 148, dated 16 July, 1968, was my ticket to war. Twelve out of the twenty eight 96B20s were assigned to the US Army security agency and further assigned to 509th Radio Research Group in the Republic of Vietnam. This included my good buddies Glenn Witt and Chuck Meniscus. On this trip to war we were allowed 135 pounds of baggage. My parents bought me a brand-new suitcase; you know the one they let the gorilla play with in the commercial? Well, that was a commercial; they should have let the US Army handle it. When I got to Bien Hoa, it had a hole in it.

In 1968, the US Army Green Uniform (dress uniform) was required on all continental United States (CONUS) travel during the winter months and the short khakis during the summer months. Armed with these orders, I was officially tasked to go to war.

The flight from Charleston, West Virginia, to San Francisco, California, was quiet and reflective. We were all in uniform. It wasn't a novelty back then. The only big difference was that we were wearing specialist 4th class rank and only one ribbon, the National Defense Service Medal, and our bolo rifle qualification badge.

San Francisco was the end of the flight. We were bussed across the Golden Gate Bridge to Oakland California. This was the highlight of my journey, traveling across the famous orange-looking bridge. I always thought of California as a beautiful paradise, with palm trees, Disney Land, and sunny beaches. However, the US Army base at Oakland was an awful place.

It was a huge base, one of the biggest I've ever visited. We were in-processed and moved to temporary barracks. We performed KP and some localized guard duty. I volunteered for pots and pans at KP. This duty was tough, but cleaning pots and pans was easier than any other job I could think of. We thought we would never get out of this place. They put us into a very large warehouse. We were processed and given a bunk in an area that housed up to six hundred troops. Whenever I watch a movie called *The Longest Day* (c. 1962), the scene where the crap game was played in a barracks area where men crammed into a large warehouse reminds me of the Oakland barracks. In the movie, hundreds of men, three bunks high, were seen waiting to load up for their airdrop into France. This large room was about the same size as the room where I was housed. Perhaps it was the same room where they shot the movie in 1960–61.

I remember pulling KP duty and pining to actually get on the airplane for a ride to Vietnam, anywhere but Oakland! Eventually we were processed for shipping out overseas, and we climbed aboard a Braniff Airline jet.

We island-hopped from Oakland to Anchorage, Alaska to Wake Island to Japan and then into Bien Hoa, Vietnam. I sent two postcards home on my way over; here is what I described on each card:

August 18, 1968: *Hi Folks, this is the type of plane I flew on to my unit; it's got just about everything on it. Everything is A-OK. I'll get to see Japan, too, so it will be a nice trip. We're at about 38,000 ft. The sun is setting way out over the Pacific. There are five girls on board, ha. Anyway, everything is A-OK, your son, Love Kenny.*

We stopped in Anchorage, Alaska. Flying into Anchorage, we were above majestic mountains. As far as the eye could see, this mountain range was capped with snow and was beautiful. After landing, I began to write another postcard:

August 19: *Hi Mom, Dad, Dave, Dana. I stopped at Alaska, and it was cool. It is too rich for me. It is pretty here; the mountains are beautiful. Japan is ok. It's pretty from the air. I have a present for you and Pam. It is pretty. We didn't get to see much of Japan, but at least I was here. We've been flying for 11 hours, everything is A-OK. Hope all are OK, too. See you later, Love Kenny.*

Continuing toward Bien Hoa, our plane stopped in Japan. I cannot remember the name of the base, but I think it was Yokota. I remember seeing Mt. Fuji from the air. The mountain towered above the clouds and was the largest land form you could see on descent into the airfield.

I didn't spend much time in Japan. I was able to walk outside and do some quick shopping, but soon the plane was refueled, and we boarded for a continuance to Bien Hoa, Republic of Vietnam.

After spending several days at Long Binh, we were convoyed to Saigon where we stayed until our assignment to the field. While in Saigon, I stayed at a hotel called the Royal Oaks Hotel in Cholon District. While at the hotel, I began to write several letters a week to my parents and brothers. Unfortunately I only have one surviving letter about the Vietnam War. My mom threw all those letters out during one of her spells where she was not thinking right. I understood her illness and didn't hold that against her. But, there are no surviving letters to my parents, save this one letter I wrote sometime in October 1969 while I was stationed at Bien Hoa.

October 1969: *Hi Mom and Dad, Dave, Dana, and little coffee drinking Cubby! Dumb dumb!*

Well, just a few lines to let you know I'm A-OK. I wrote to Grandpa tonight, and I'll write Pop tomorrow night. I didn't tell him where I was, I don't think I should worry him none. Oh yea, before I forget, do you think you could send me an artificial Christmas tree? I'll send you the money. I know it might sound dumb, but it will give us guys something to look forward to. I think we can get the lights we need over here. Anyway, let me know how much they are.

So far your mail has been real regular. Haven't heard from hardly anybody, but it takes a while to get started I guess.

I'm hoping for my Spc. 5 in or around March, I should get it over here, and if I try real hard, I can probably make either Spc. 6 or Sgt. E-6, but that's to be seen. I want to make it so bad I can taste it! Ha.

It's raining tonight (which is bad, means it could rain forever! Ha), but it's a soft, quiet type of rain. The kind we get at home. Good for crops.

Mommason brought me some fruit the other day, looked like pig you know whats, but inside, the fruit was like a grape! But tasted like beechnut gum, real good, too. I guess it's because I gave her some cookies.

Tomorrow we have a general inspecting our hotel. So, I've cleaned up our room. He'll probably laugh when he walks in; it's just as roomy as home. (I don't plan to be here, though!)

I think I'm going to miss hunting! Seems like it should start getting cold, but it's getting hotter. I guess you heard what "Westy" Westmoreland said; we might be home by '70. He says the ARVN Army is getting stronger, and they are. They do their share now; sometimes they are lazy but not all of them. There are quite a few Australians, Filippinos, and Thailanders here; they are pretty interesting to watch. Also there are some others, I think New Zealand, and a couple others are here; they fight, too. So the US isn't alone.

Well, best go for now, I'll write later. Keep those cards and letters coming.

Love Kenny
P.S. How old is Dana's teacher? Haha

I am surprised at what a young man will write about when he's twenty one years old and away from home. I had visited Dana's class room when I was home for my thirty day leave, all of September 1969.

One side story to tell here is during one of the rainstorms during August 1968, the Saigon River overflowed. This was the monsoon season, and Saigon received seventeen inches of rain. The next morning when I awoke, my "flip flops" were floating around the room in about two feet of water.

Out in the hall, fish were swimming up and down the hall! The water stayed up for most of the morning, and eventually was pumped out by the early afternoon. The Royal Oaks was constantly pumping water out of the shallow parts of the building into a large holding pond in front of the hotel. Kids would come swim in that hole every day, and it was a choke point to our hotel which made a ground assault a little more difficult. There was a daytime guard on the front entrance, and at night there were additional sentries on guard on the roof.

While upstairs on the roof at night, overlooking the city, you could hear gunfire erupt from many parts of the city. Sometimes you could hear and feel B-52 arc lite strikes where hundreds of 2000-pound bombs were dropped on some enemy position near the city. Our hotel would shake and sway like an earthquake. Closer to our hotel, we could spy rats, about the size of a normal house cat in this country, swimming along the small channel of water behind the hotel. We always kept soda cans filled with water and would "bomb" them from several stories up, trying to kill one for spite.

Out behind the hotel was a huge area built up with pieces of cardboard, plywood, tarmac, and anything people could find. Houses were just shanties, and whole families lived there. Saigon was so crowded by refugees from the war that it overwhelmed the government's ability to help people. This destroyed-and-rebuilt area had been destroyed when the Viet Cong came into the Cholon area and tried to overrun the hotels and kill all the Americans. My room, right above my bed, was pockmarked by machine gun or automatic weapons fire. As occupants of the hotel, the 509th issued us weapons, even though we could not work yet because our clearances were being completed for a special security code word intelligence access.

Hotel life was boring except for an occasional firefight or explosion in Saigon. The water we showered in came from a cistern on top of the roof. It was heated by sunlight. If you stayed in the shower too long, the water got cold! Also, the water, which smelled nasty, wasn't fit to drink. We brushed our teeth in it, but it tasted like oily, muddy, mucky water.

During the day, Chuck, Glenn and I went into Tan Son Nhut airbase to the 509th Radio Research Group headquarters at Davis Station. We would check on our clearances and mess around in their day room. We kept asking when can we go to work and received the same answer, "When your clearance arrives." After spending most of the day waiting on news we eventually left and flagged down a single-seat moped taxi. The idea was get us back to the hotel as fast as possible. Each one of us would pull out a dollar and tell the driver, "If you beat those other two back to our hotel, I'll double this" whereupon we all took off at high speed, weaving in and out of traffic. That was the highlight of the day.

We carried loaded M-14 rifles everywhere we went in Saigon. Sporadic shootings and assassinations and bombings happened every day. One afternoon, on our way to dinner, we were walking down the main street. Traffic was heavy, and cars were hurriedly going in both directions. Across the street, some GIs parked their deuce and half truck in front of a bar. We assumed they were inside drinking, but outside a whole host of people were stealing items out of their truck. At once, all three of us yelled and pulled our rifles off our shoulders. I took a bead on one of the teens on the back of a motor bike with a small box in his hands. I yelled, "Halt," but he gave me the Vietnamese finger, and they sped off. I stopped traffic when I lowered the rife on the motorbike, and like a Spaghetti Western, the people loafing along the store fronts scattered.

One little boy, about four, was stealing a speaker. It was probably bigger than him and much heavier. I chased him around the corner of a building. At a full gallop, he threw the speaker up in the air and it came down, hitting him in the head as it fell to the ground. I stopped chasing him and picked up the speaker and took it back to the truck. My first contact with the enemy was less than stellar.

Chuck guarded the truck as Glenn and I looked for the truck driver. We found them having a beer, and we told them they had been ransacked. They rushed outside, but the damage was done. They lost most of their valuables, and we had terrorized most of Cholon district. I guess that was "ops normal" for Saigon.

As new soldiers in country, the local people tried all the old tricks on us to take our valuables or steal our watches. I bought a watch that had a wristband that used a buckle instead of a flexible wrist band. The flexible wrist bands would allow kids to strip your watch off your arm and run away before you could catch them. My brand-new watch my grandfather gave me for graduation rusted off my wrist and fell off, sliding into a city gutter in Saigon. I stepped off the bus one day, and zip, it broke flying off my wrist and sliding down a sewer. It was gone.

The city was overcrowded, and GIs were easy pickings. Pickpockets, ladies of the night, and a whole host of people were always after your valuables. One day, I hailed a cab for a trip to Ton Son Nhut to check mail and check on our clearances. I was alone. I made a big mistake of getting into a cab with two people up front, the driver and another person. This is a grave error in any foreign country. You never get into a cab with another person sitting up front in the cab. It's a big personal risk.

As soon as I entered the cab, the man sitting beside the driver said, "We can take you to his sister; she is number one."

I retorted, "No, I need to go to Ton Son Nhut. I don't want to see your sister or anyone else."

Again he insisted and the driver chimed in, "Yes that's where we are going."

I chambered a round in the M-14 and slammed the bolt shut. Flipping off the safety and putting my finger on the trigger, I stuck the gun into the neck of the driver. I said, "Take me to Ton Son Nhut now, or I'm going to blow your head off!"

At that point, they shut up except for talking in Vietnamese.

I never took the rifle off his neck until we arrived outside the gate of Ton Son Nhut Air Base. I exited the taxi, keeping my rifle on them. They yelled at me because I did not pay them. I backed off toward the gate, and the MPs ran out to see what was going on. I told them and they waved that taxi off. I really felt a sigh of relief; it was the dumbest thing I had done in my entire life. I would not make that mistake again.

There was a PX not far from our hotel, and I enjoyed shopping for necessities and sodas. So far I was waiting on a clearance that seemed to take forever to arrive, but eventually it came through. In October 1968, we were directed to the personnel section of the 509th Radio Research Group Headquarters. As we walked in and were getting processed, the sergeant major asked us where we had been. "Where were you guys?"

"At the motel waiting, like we were told," was the answer.

"What did you do?" he asked.

Well, we didn't lie so we told him, "We pulled guard duty and changed light bulbs and helped with odd jobs. We couldn't hang around the base because we didn't have a clearance."

At this he tore into a rant and read us the riot act. "Send these men to the field. I don't care if they get killed; send them out to the field." That is how Chuck ended up with the Radio Research Detachment with the 1st Cav, and Glenn and I ended up at the 175th Radio Research Company, II Field Force, as 96B20 combat intelligence analysts at Bien Hoa, about twenty-five or more miles north of Saigon. It was a huge target, and we became residents of Rocket City, or "Rocket Alley," as it was called.

Chapter 7

THE 175TH RADIO RESEARCH COMPANY—OCTOBER 1968

I f you google a 1968 map of Bien Hoa, you would find the 175th Radio Research unit on the northern perimeter of Bien Hoa army base next to Lassiter helicopter pad about 1000 meters north and east of the main Bien Hoa Runway that ran east and west. Our unit was spread parallel to the northern perimeter. We manned eight or nine bunkers from the L-shaped indentation on the northern perimeter to the gun emplacements on our right flank. These guns were 175mm howitzers, and eight-inch guns that lit up the sky at night and gave an ear-shattering KAABOOOM.

The unit work area was an old metal building, quite large with ceiling fans and no air conditioning. We had box fans in our work areas, but the heat was so brutal that we were allowed to work in T-shirts. One of the unit members visited the area recently and said he thought the building was now used to make hats for Vietnam veterans. There is irony there somewhere.

We were shelled my very first night at work. We scrambled for the bunker and crawled into the darkness. Shells were coming closer, passed over us, and went down the road from north to south. They turned east and finally to a spot where a volley of shells were lobbed at us. These were mortars. Sitting in the bunker, I learned my first lesson: rockets were less predictable than mortars which are more accurate. The enemy used a spotter to help their mortar crews "walk" the mortars down the street and left to the 11th Armored Cav tactical operations center. The VC spotter would relay information to an enemy mortar team that was relatively close. They would adjust their mortar tube and fire another mortar until the target was hit, then dissolve into the jungle. The sounds of this attack were one I will never forget.

Our unit was assigned to the 303rd RR Battalion, II Field Force, Vietnam. II Field Force was a Corps-size unit. It arrived in Vietnam on 15 March 1966. According to historians, the II FFV Vietnam traced its history back to XXII US Army

Corps that was formed in 1944 in the European campaign and inactivated after World War II. It was reactivated at Fort Hood, Texas, and renamed the II Field Force during the Vietnam War.

The II Field Force had the following units assigned to it during the war: 1st, 9th, and 25th Infantry Divisions; The 101st and 82nd Airborne Divisions; 173rd Airmobile Brigade; 1st Cavalry Division; 11th Armored Cavalry Regiment, 12th Combat Aviation Group, 23rd and 54th Artillery Groups, the 1st Australian Task Force (Vung Tau), and Royal Thai Army Volunteer Force (Bear Cat). And, of course, the 175th Radio Research Company was stationed at Bien Hoa.

As you entered the compound, there was a sign that stated the unit motto "First In and Last Out." In reality, that was a very true statement. The unit was the first intelligence unit into Vietnam and was the last unit to leave Vietnam.

The 175th Radio Research Company was labeled a "radio repair" company by some GIs who were not familiar with the unit. The acronym 175RRC was thought to be the 175th Rest and Relaxation Company. One member of our unit told the local artillerymen that the big gray operations building was a huge beer warehouse and all those "vans" parked along the side of the building were refrigeration trucks holding all the beer issued in III and IV Corps. Somehow, I think they believed him. The vans were actually used for radio intercepts.

Beyond the sign was the officer's barracks, the library and day room on the right. On the left was the CO and first sergeant's office. No one ever wanted to visit the first sergeant because that meant you were in serious trouble. I was in that office maybe three times. Checking in, checking out, and when I was in trouble.

Beyond the first few barracks, or hooches, was the club located on the left. Beyond the club was a putt-putt course. It was in bad repair and was taken down right after my arrival, just my luck. That was also the location of a large screen and projection booth. Every night there was a different movie, and if you had time or felt like it, you could catch the early movie or the late movie. You brought your own chair, and after the movie, you cleaned up your trash and took your chair to your hooch.

Beyond this was an open space of about twenty-five yards. The next building was the dining hall. It was open twenty-four hours a day and served four meals a day. We had swing shifts of twelve to eighteen hours. If you worked noon until midnight, you did that for a week. On Sunday, you shifted six hours to a 6:00 p.m. until 6:00 a.m. shift, and so forth. We never had a day off in the time I worked at the 175th Radio Research Company (RRC).

The meals at our dining hall were not so bad. Once you got over the green eggs and green ham (packed in formaldehyde), you got used to it. There were meals where we swore up and down that the meat listed as "roast beef" was really local water buffalo or maybe even road kill, monkey meat, or even dog meat. But one thing we knew, we pretended it was good old roast beef. Well, at least that's what we thought. Mystery meat remained just that, a mystery.

The dining hall was a great place to visit your coworkers, but I think the club was more active when it came to socializing. It was very small, but seemed to house a lot of people. We had a well-stocked club, with plenty of beer, booze, and sodas as well as plenty of popcorn or snacks. The club was cherished by everyone.

Down the street toward the front gate, on the right as you were going south to the gate, was a hamburger stand. Here you could get a hamburger

(more mystery meat) or a hot dog. We would fre-
quent that stand if we missed a meal or were on
our way to the PX.

Further west, towards the helicopter pad, was
a line of hooches to the right and our motor pool
was to the left. Beyond that was a back street and
then the helicopter pad. Helicopters flew twenty-four hours a day. Hundreds of sorties lifted off
that pad, and our hooch was probably half a foot-
ball field away. Noise was a constant companion
at the 175 RRC.

Between each hooch was a bunker, half of a
thirty-six-inch culvert laid on sand bags with at
least two rows of bags covering the entire length
of the culvert, about 15 feet. There was a piece
of tarmac for the floor and a row of sandbags on
either side to sit on. Since most rocket attacks came
at night, we spent a lot of time in the bunker in our
underwear. I often thought how awful it would be
to die in your boxer shorts. To be honest, we didn't
dwell on friendly deaths during these attacks.
Usually in a large rocket attack, someone would
be killed. After a while, you became numb to that
scared feeling, and sometimes you would just lay
on the floor or roll under a bunk. You didn't really
care if you were killed because you figured you

were dead anyway. I think this was very common in Vietnam until the last thirty days of your tour. Then you became paranoid about dying.

At the unit motor pool, I received training on the jeep, ¾ ton truck, and the deuce and a half truck. In each vehicle I climbed in, started the vehicle, drove it forward and backward, and shut it off. I found out where the oil stick was and took a test on international road signs. I received my first driver's license ever, a military license. After this brief driving test, I was allowed to drive a big deuce and a half all over Vietnam if I wanted. Of course, it was always scary driving anywhere in Vietnam.

On my first trip back to Saigon as the guard on a deuce and half truck, I saw my first awful traffic accident. An ARVN soldier was run over by a steam roller and flattened. This included his bike. I thought and wondered, *How on earth,* but had to shake that out of my mind. Vehicles had to be guarded or protected from grenades being slid into your gas tank, sometimes with a rubber band around the handle and the pin pulled. As soon as the fuel dissolved the rubber band it released the handle and the grenade would go off.

One of the first trips to Saigon after the Mini TET of 1969, our driver decided to take a shortcut in Cholon. We turned off the main road, and the big truck eased down a narrow lane, its diesel engine breaking the silence of the area. About half a mile down this very narrow road, the road split and became even narrower. Barely fitting between buildings, the driver continued until it became impassable. Only bicycles and mopeds could go further, and he shouted back to us, "I need to back out. You guys run point for me and help me get out of here."

He started backing up the mile or two we were down this corridor. All the houses had balconies with people now leaning over to see what the ruckus was. Walking with M-14 locked and loaded, we figured we were going to get a grenade tossed into the bed of the truck. Eventually, we backed to a turnaround spot, and we vacated the area. We had no business back there, and it was embarrassing.

On one courier trip to Long Binh, I was returning with my secrets locked in the back of the ¾ ton truck I was driving in the left lane of a four-lane highway. I was shadowed and eventually pulled over by a US military policeman in a jeep.

I shut off the engine and showed him my driver's license. He told me I was driving in the left lane too much and that he was going to give me a ticket. I was surprised because the right lane had all these slower Lambretta scooters, motorcycles, and what not, in the way. The left lane was the only lane useable, and I was in a hurry to secure secrets. Finally he let me go, and I was astonished that I was even stopped. I guess he was bored.

Every day we couriered top secret classified material from Bien Hoa to Long Binh, a seven mile trip one way. This special mail was on its way to the director of the National Security Agency (DIRNSA). I worked with a Spc4. Thompson, who was a bitter young man, hated the Army and hated what was going on in the United States even worse. We would double-wrap the secret stuff, stamping designs on the inner wrappings with the secret stamp. I got pretty good at drawing Snoopy with the SECRET stamp, quite impressive. However, we received a lot of hate mail from DIRNSA! We figured, what the heck, what are they going to do—send us to Vietnam? After several months of working in the mail room, I was finally assigned as an order of Battle analyst. It took a while to work into the section.

Everything we recorded and kept on file was done by pencil on 3 × 5 or 5 × 8 card-stock. Notes on units went back years, and meticulous notes were kept on all the Viet Cong and the increasing North Vietnamese Army divisions. We also kept notes on regiments, and battalions, commanders, and strength, disposition, tactics, training, weapons, and Order of Battle. OB was a line and block chart showing just what units made up a regiment or the division. We created our own daily intelligence summary and we gave a daily morning briefing to the operations officer and the unit commander.

I kept a large map of III and IV Corps showing locations of collateral and signals intelligence information. Collateral information was battle-field reports used to place enemy locations on my map. I also used signals intelligence showing locations of the same unit. This helped with developing enemy courses of action. Sometimes looking at a familiar pattern of movement might signal which friendly unit was the possible target of an attack. More than once our analysis sent to Saigon ended up in the newspapers as "sources quoted"; we were those sources.

One day Spc. 4 Pat M. bought a Thompson 45 caliber sub-machine gun and one clip of ammo for fifty dollars. He had three bullets for his clip. On one of our trips to Long Binh, to deliver classified mail, Pat rode along with me as my guard. I was pretty sore at him for bringing the Thompson instead of his 45 caliber pistol and his M-14 rifle. We briefly argued, but I decided to take my pistol and rifle along, just in case. Somewhere between Long Binh and Bien Hoa, Pat shot his Thompson twice into high banks of earth along the road. Now he had one bullet left. When we arrived at Long Binh, I left Pat outside in my ¾ ton truck.

While inside, I delivered the secrets and wrote out my briefing I was taking back for our commander. When I came back to the truck, Pat was sitting in the rear seat of a military police jeep, handcuffed. This upset me, and I started mouthing off at the MP. "Damn it, you can't arrest my guard, I'm an official US courier. What the hell is wrong with you!"

Whereupon the MP looked me in the eye and said, "Some guard you got. He had one bullet left in that machine gun, and he used that one bullet to shoot a hole in your roof." He pointed at my truck. Sure enough, Pat had shot a hole in the roof of my truck, crap! So, I talked them into letting Pat ride back with me, holding my M-14 and they agreed, but would follow us to the company area to file a report to Major Ferking, our commander.

I told Pat, "When we get to Ops, you jump out and go through the operations gate, get your badge from our MPs and keep on going inside. I'll follow you."

That's what we did, leaving our MP escort bewildered at the front gate of the top secret intelligence operations building. They filed their complaint with Major Ferking. Pat and I got yelled at, but that was about the extent of what the good major did to us. We were lucky. Pat's Thompson was confiscated, and he lost his money. That was a lot better than going to Long Binh jail for a few weeks. In addition, Pat had to pay for the truck roof replacement.

Vietnam has a preponderance of monkeys. Monkeys live in the jungle and end up being sold on the streets of Vietnam as pets. One day, a young boy brought his pet monkey to our barracks. We paid him twenty-five cents each to clean out our barracks of spiders. He promptly opened the door and released his monkey. Deftly climbing up the wall to the rafters, the monkey ate every single spider it could get its hands on. Cramming his mouth full of spiders, the monkey constantly chewed and chased spiders until he had traversed the entire length of our building. Eventually, with his stomach full, the monkey returned to the young boy, and they went on their merry way to the next hooch.

Wild animals roamed outside the wire on the perimeter of major US installations. Often, you would see a water buffalo or boa constrictors or even tigers. You never knew exactly what was out beyond those five fences. One evening the Special Forces guys brought in an eighteen-foot-long boa constrictor. Big and fat, they ran over it with their jeep, jumped out, and shot it in the head. No one liked guard duty on the perimeter. You would stare out of the bunker window, and every dark stump would move. For all you knew, the enemy was out there watching you looking for him.

It was on a quiet and very dark night that I had my encounter with one of Vietnam's wild animals. Besides the pit vipers, rats, scorpions and huge mosquitoes, not much else would inhabit our bunkers. No one slept inside those bunkers; it was too darn dark and uncomfortable. So, two men would sleep outside while the third man watched for the enemy out the bay window of the bunker.

At about 2:00 a.m. (I really cannot remember the exact time), in the wee hours of the morning, I was sitting on a stool staring out into total darkness. Earlier that evening, we had opened up our "B" rations of canned meat, peanut butter (packed sometime during WWII) and crackers. We had opened those rations with P-38 can openers, ate the contents, and then we tossed the cans over the berm into "no-man's land." We found out later that was a big mistake!

So, early in the morning, and staring out into pure total blackness, my mind is trying to stay focused. However, when you're alone and in total darkness, your mind will wander back to home, and eventually to girls. You'll eventually shake that off and go back to doing what you're supposed to be doing, and that is looking for Charlie VC.

At night, every stump looks like the enemy. Every bush seems to be moving; it can make the hair on the back of your neck stand up. It was in this environment that suddenly something stood up directly in front of me. It was on top of me and my M-60 machine gun before I could react. Darn, an attack! Face-to-face with this enemy, I reacted quickly. Letting out a blood-curdling scream, I fell backward off the stool. As I fell back, I remember seeing a little monkey doing a complete back flip, landing on all fours, and running madly away.

The two troopers asleep outside thought I had been stabbed, and they flew into the bunker with rifles ready. On the ground and struggling to get up, I was cursing. My buddy was yelling, "What's wrong; what the hell happened?"

I replied, "It was a darn monkey that scared the hell out of me!" There was a period of quietness, some call it a pregnant moment. Then both men gave a groan and went back to their cots outside. With my pride and backside hurting, I re-assumed the position of guard, praying that nothing else would scare the dickens out of me for the rest of the night.

On another moonlit night, the officer of the day (OD) jeep was creeping toward our bunker. I was carrying the M-79 grenade launcher with a 40mm buckshot round. It was like loading a huge shotgun shell that shot more than a dozen buck-shot-sized balls in a spray pattern. I stopped the jeep and challenged the lieutenant and his visitor, a nurse. "Halt! Who goes there?" I barked.

"Lieutenant so and so," he replied.

"Advance and be recognized," I said in my military monotone. He advanced, and we exchanged passwords. He immediately chewed me out for using the M-79 grenade launcher as a challenge weapon. I thought it was a perfect weapon with the buckshot round. He didn't.

He never introduced the nurse who was with him. She was dressed in an all-white nurse's outfit. She was an officer, too, and didn't say much. He ordered me to replace my shotgun round with a 40mm anti-personnel round. I did and made sure the weapon was safe before handing it over to him. He took the grenade launcher and climbed the pushed-up berm, denude of plants, because of the defoliant used to spray the perimeter.

Now, what happened next was a series of events that I will never forget to my dying day. He was explaining to the nurse how to use of the M-79. How it was used as an anti-personnel weapon and was usually shot using Kentucky windage. He had his arms around her as he helped her nestle the launcher to her shoulder. His soft-spoken sweet tone to her was causing me to giggle inside. *What a ham*, I thought. He stepped back, and I saw she was going to fire the grenade into no man's land.

I spied her feet. They were side by side — she was not poised for the weapon recoil.

She pulled the trigger and the "THUNK" of the grenade launcher sent a shell out into the tree-less scrub in front of us. I don't think she ever saw the grenade hit the ground. As soon as she pulled the trigger, the recoil of the M-79 knocked her backward, and she slid all the way down to the bottom of that red clay earthen berm on her back. She got up and noticed her whites were streaked with red clay from north to south. She let out a scream and started dusting herself off. He was trying to help, but the red stain wasn't budging. "How am I going to explain this?" she said in an aggravating tone. I don't think he said a word, but hurried her back to the jeep, after handing me the grenade launcher. I reloaded my grenade launcher with a buckshot shell as they drove out of sight. She was still screaming at him. He was trying to shush her, to no avail. For a long moment, all was quiet. The jeep droned out of sight, and the three of us looked at each other. In my most sarcastic voice I muttered, "Bet he don't get none of that tonight." We all laughed and snickered and went back to doing our duty.

When the base was thinking it might be under surveillance or a ground attack, we would be ordered to do a "mad minute." This order meant that you could shoot whatever ordnance you had into no man's land to see if there was a response. You shot everything you owned for one minute and then ceased fire. At Bien Hoa, there were no responses, but the enemy and your own Special Forces were always just beyond the last fence, moving around. VC spider holes, a small hole dug straight down in the ground where a single VC could hide, were common near the base perimeter. Even VC radio squawks were intercepted not far from the base. Usually, this meant the enemy had conducted a surveillance for an attack.

The perimeter at night can be a nerve-racking, albeit boring, place to be. If you were on guard duty, you usually missed the midnight meal. Sometimes the mess hall would supplement the B-rations with some sandwiches. One night, a ¾ ton truck sneaked its way along the perimeter road, stopping at each bunker and tower. The driver had brought each soldier a couple of ham sandwiches and iced-down Coca Cola. That was the best meal I had in all eighteen months in Vietnam.

Sometimes you were at the right place at the right time to witness something incredible. My hooch was about two hooches away from Lassiter field, a helicopter pad. Helicopters took off day and night, twenty-four hours a day, seven days a week. A helicopter taking off in the early afternoon didn't seem to affect us, nor did we pay it much attention.

We were playing Frisbee in our skivvies, just our boxer shorts, outside our hooch. We were passing it back and forth, getting some sun and working off some stress before cleaning up. I heard something metallic hit the tarmac, and it ricocheted over the perimeter and out of sight in seconds. This was very unusual, so all of us looked over at the field at the same instant. A helicopter was beginning to rotate around and around; it had lost its tail rotor. Finally the pilot crash-landed into the tarmac and broke down the struts. He shut down the engine, and no one was hurt, but the helicopter appeared to be bent and broken. Somehow he had lost his J nut that holds the tail rotor on the aircraft, and that resulted in a crash landing using auto rotation. Apparently, no one was injured, and we had witnessed a helicopter crash. Just one of those things you witness that happens quickly, and later you shake your head and say out loud, "Holy Cow."

A second remarkable event that happened to many soldiers in Vietnam was meeting someone you graduated with just walking by you or getting on another helicopter for parts unknown. This happened more often than you would think, considering there were well over 580,000 men in Vietnam.

Walking toward our unit operations area, I passed someone going the other direction. I glanced up at the person briefly, and I did a double take. When he looked back at me, I recognized Jim Cole from Nitro, West Virginia! I was stunned, and we shook hands and marveled that we found each other thousands of miles away from Nitro. Jim came back to the hooch, and we talked about our experiences. Jim was heading home, and I was just starting my adventure. But for one brief moment in history, time stood still. To this very day, I feel that Jim is one of my brothers, truly someone I could talk to and lean on in hard times when I needed some mental shoring up. Many veterans have had this happen, and they all speak of these encounters as I do with almost a reverence for the person and the meeting. Perhaps it is something psychologists should study, or perhaps they already have a good name for it—homecoming. Looking back all these years later, I am amazed at how close some of my high school buddies were, many within just a few miles of Bien Hoa and less than an hour's drive away.

Jim related a story to me about his duty with the 1st Cav at Quan Lou:

It was a scary place because they were just building up the green line defense. In some places we just had one or two rows of wire. I remember one night on guard duty, the officer of the day came around and asked if everybody had enough ammo. This one guy answered, "Sir, I have plenty of ammo, but only two magazines." The officer said, "How you going to get by like that?" He answered, "Sir I am a fast loader." true story. (James Cole, email 2017).

II Field Force Patch. We didn't wear intelligence
brass or the ASA patch.

My first photo in uniform at Fort Knox, Kentucky. Age 19.

Picture of lining up in our squad during basic training.
Fort Knox, Kentucky. January to March, 1968.

On top of the Royal Oaks Hotel overlooking Cholon
district. First picture taken in Saigon, August 1968.

U.S. Embassy building with patched bullet holes,
August 1968.

Buddhist Funeral procession. Saigon, September 1968.

Arrived 175th Radio Research Company, Bien Hoa Army Base, Republic of Vietnam. Early October 1968.

Another angle of our company area showing hooches and mess hall. We had 24 hour a day mess hall chow.

A blown up view of an aircraft spraying the base. They sprayed both agent orange on the perimeter and mosquito control.

Our Operations building. One of our members told the artillery battery next to us that we stored all the beer for Vietnam in that building.

Our outdoor theater where ìBarbarellaî and ìThe Yellow Submarineî premiered.

The northern perimeter looking into ìno mans land.î Bien Hoa was protected with five fences. Enemy forces were always just outside our wire at night.

Another view from the guard tower. Showing the mortar pit used to illuminate the night if intruders were near or in the wire.

In front of the bunker laying out five claymore mines. Note the lack of grass in this area. Additional truck spraying of defoliant kept grass from growing.

This bunker was protected from enemy RPG 7 and possible mortar rounds. Note sandbags stacked at least five or six layers on the roof.

My M-14 rifle and gear used on the perimeter.

Me at age 20, just before turning 21 and the Mini Tet of February, 1969.

The last fence of triple strand concertina wire before the berm protecting the base.

Buddhist Temple overlooking Bien Hoa Air Base. This site was used as an observation and location of Bien Hoa infrastructure by the Viet Cong.

M-60 machine gun, usually with 1000 rounds, was issued to each bunker. Three rifle men, with their M-14's, and one carrying an M-79 Grenade launcher and 40 rounds. I usually carried 11 clips of 7.62mm ammo on the berm.

M-79 grenade launcher had to be used outside of the bunker. Firing inside could cause the grenade to bounce off the overhang and explode in front of you.

Downtown Bien Hoa, a small village near the Song Dong Nai river.

A local civilian bus on the main highway along Long Binh.
This area was considered a weakness by the Viet Cong.
They had no respect for cooks, clerks, and rear area people.
They figured they would overrun us and then
feast on our rations.

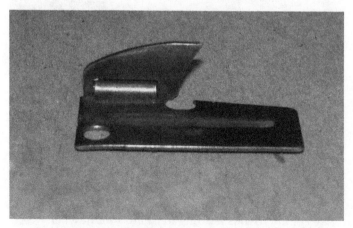

P-38 can opener. This little device was issued to most
everyone in the 5th Viet Cong Division. They were going
to use this to eat our rations after over running
us and killing everyone.

This was our immediate cover from rocket and mortar attacks. Sharing this spot with snakes and rats gave most of us an uneasy feeling.

Two of my friends heading to Guard Mount where we were told the current intelligence by the officer in charge. Of course, we wrote the narrative so we could recite it by heart. We could not tell anyone we were the authors of that information.

Me and ìShakeyî dog. Our three legged dog that was our company mascot. He was protected and loved by everyone that met him.

This is Glenn Whit from Alabama. He's petting ìMister.î This short haired white dog would let you pet him about three times before he bit you. We always had fun with the new guys.

This was Bien Hoa's Best protection. The 11th Armored Cavalry, ìBlack Horseî regiment was headquartered at Bien Hoa army base. One of the best fighting units in Vietnam. This is an M-113 armored personnel carrier with a mesh fence used to capture or stop a Rocket Propelled Grenade.

M-48 tank used by the 11th ACR in tight quarters and jungle terrain. Using our Intelligence Colonel Patton stationed his fighting units to effectively counterattack the 5th VC Division.

Everyone in this farm house were murdered during the February, 1969, attack on Bien Hoa.

A typical farm near Bien Hoa. All of these farmers and Bien Hoa residents fled the VC attack. Some were captured, some murdered.

Helicopter in bunker at Lassiter Field, near my hooch.

Long Range Reconnaissance Patrol (LRRP) unloading
at Lassiter.

Rocket slamming into buildings just behind our motor pool area. Subsequent fire burnt the building down.

Train derailment from VC attack on the rail system to cut the road between Long Binh and Bien Hoa. February 1969.

107mm Rocket slammed into Lassiter Helicopter pad.
The nose of the rocket buried itself into the tarmac.

Pictured shared by a colleague showing damage to
buildings near Bien Hoa. The battle lasted from the 19
to the 27th of February, 1969.

Ho Nai orphanage entrance. One of two projects our unit under took in Vietnamization plan. The other project was the Bien Hoa mental hospital.

Glenn Whit with Vietnamese orphans. They embraced us as Dads.

The orphans are visiting our company area before the TET of 1969 offensive. They are leading us to the club to put on their cultural dances.

Little girls, and one little boy, did the ribbon dance.

Hung is eating a meal with us. I tried to see if my parents could adopt her, but her mother was alive and Vietnamese law prohibited adoption.

Finally home in March of 1970.

Chapter 8

WELCOME TO ROCKET ALLEY– BIEN HOA 1968 TO 1969

The name "Rocket Alley" was well coined. We took rockets, and mortars so often that I lost count how many actually impacted the base during my year tour. I quit counting after hundreds of rounds hit the base, there were just too many rounds. The 175th Radio Research Company was staffed with men who had committed themselves to four years of military service. The Army Security Agency (ASA) added military intelligence types (MI) order of battle (OB) specialists to their work centers. This created an awkward situation. Order of Battle specialists, MOS of 96B20, were three-year enlistees. We were trained to study and analyze battle field intelligence. ASA men were trained to collect and study signals intelligence.

After a little chiding from the ASA folks, life for me finally settled down into a routine.

Partitions separated the work areas inside our Operations building. A small room in the back of our building was air conditioned. It housed our large crypto teletype machines. I could use various machines tied to different locations in Vietnam using a secret scrambled link. In 1968 this was as close to the internet as we had. It was primitive, to today's standards, but served us well. If an area of Vietnam was under attack we could communicate via teletype with their analysts. This gave us a quick insight as to what was happening. There was no such thing as a day off. On top of my daily work, I pulled guard duty on the perimeter, or in the tower, once a week. Every day I drove a truck filled with secrets to Long Binh to the 303rd RRBn.

We were fortunate to have an outside movie location. Movies were shown on a large screen of three 4 × 8 pieces of plywood that were painted white. Our movie projector was a 16mm Bell and Howell that was a true workhorse! Movies were shown at 7 p.m. (or right after dusk) and midnight. The outside movie theater was located near our club. Beer and pretzels were only a few steps away. But it was bring your own chair.

Each night, about thirty minutes prior to a movie, everyone would show up with their lounge chair, a couple of beers, and some snacks and would settle down to chit chat prior to the movie starting. This was a social time when soldiers read mail or discussed cars and girls, and it was actually a great way to ease stress.

On two occasions, this tranquil scene was unexpectedly disturbed. The first time our theater was disrupted was during the showing of a movie called the *Yellow Submarine*. Now all us GIs had heard about this latest Beatles movie, but no one had ever *seen* the movie. So, at dusk the projector started to roll. Lo and behold, the *Yellow Submarine* is a stupid cartoon. Frankly, it is a stupid movie!

We always shared our movies with neighbors. We were the in-processing area for the 101st Air Mobile Division, and eventually the 1st Cavalry Division. Our unit shared our club, our library, and movies, even though on some occasions they teargassed our sleeping area for meanness.

This night was no different; the 1st Cav men shared our movie, and we all settled down as one happy band of brothers to watch another funny Beatles movie. About five minutes into the *Yellow Submarine*, the cartoon movie, was getting the best of everyone. A beer can hit the screen. Pow! Beer flew everywhere. It seems the grunts were extremely unhappy with a stupid cartoon movie about four long-haired idiots! I agreed, but then our macho guys bowed up.

Our unit had a detachment of MPs assigned to it. The head MP sergeant stood up, stopped the movie, and walked to the front of the screen. He said, in his command voice, "Any son-of-a-bitch that throws another beer can is going to get his ass whipped!" About one second after that speech, about one hundred beer cans came flying toward the screen. In an instant, a great fight broke out between infantrymen of the 1st Cav and Rear Area Mother F's of the 175th. We had some pretty rough-and-tough guys ourselves, but I wasn't one of them! Ducking down, I crawled out of the melee and retreated to a safe distance to watch about a hundred men beat each other until the blood flowed. The fight finally stopped when helmeted police showed up with side arms!

I thought that I would never see anything so strange at a movie showing until the movie *Barbarella* showed up. Now *Barbarella* was a dumb sci-fi movie about a girl that went around half naked fighting aliens. I think that's what it's about.

All the GIs thought that Jane Fonda was a hot chick. She was a good-looking lady, and all of us were quite excited to get this showing of a movie that showed a little skin! According to rumor, Jane Fonda shows up with her breasts bared, and of course, being GIs, who would miss that? This was way before she visited North Vietnam.

So, the movie was started at dusk. The sun was down, and we were well into this sci-fi movie when it happened. The base siren went off. Immediately all of us knew we had seconds to find cover. Dashing for the bunker behind the chow hall, only thirty yards away, I was knocked down by a 122mm rocket (millimeter being its diameter) slamming into our company motor pool area. It was the first time I was knocked down by the concussion of a rocket hitting nearby. Slightly dazed and scared, I was lying in a little rivulet, or gully, made by the water flow from a gutter spout from the chow hall. I tried to get my butt as low as possible.

Rockets were popping all over the base, and I wondered if I was going to catch shrapnel lying out in an open, sandy area. I looked over my shoulder, and there playing was *Barbarella*. No one was watching. All that was left was a jumble of empty chairs strewn all about. In a way, I think it was poetic justice that none of us got to see Jane Fonda's breasts. To this day, I have not seen Jane Fonda's breasts or that movie or any movie that Jane Fonda ever acted in.

It's unfortunate for her that she went to North Vietnam and wore that red dress all over Hanoi. Every GI was quite in love with her until she committed treason with the North Vietnamese. Those who served in Vietnam will never forgive Jane Fonda's bad behavior in Hanoi.

On the day of Neil Armstrong's moon walk in 1969, that July night, we were hit twice by a barrage of 122mm rockets — twelve to twenty-five rockets smacked into the base. These attacks killed several GIs. I guess they wanted to share in our proud moment, too. I'm surprised they didn't try a perimeter probe.

I never dreamed I would undergo a field inspection in Vietnam, but I did. We had to clean our rifles and slings, clean our canteens and mess kits (we never used the mess kits, but we had them anyway), bayonet, poncho, battle rattle belt, flashlight, and so on. It had to be displayed a certain way, and all had to be the same. I think this was in response to an incident we had one night when the unit was told to remove all their interior plywood barriers, and the hooch became an open barracks again. The men piled all their lumber up into one huge pile and burned it, causing a great fire in the middle of the barren field between lines of hooches. So now we were having a field inspection. The army has a template they use; if the soldiers grumble, then give them an inspection. I think it works.

The major and a sergeant major were conducting the inspection. As the major walked into the barracks, he noticed "Rat" R. (his nickname) had a piece of red tape around the end of his muzzle. The major stopped. "What's this son?" he queried. Rat replied, "I cannot remember my rifle serial number, but this red tape helps me find my rifle quickly." I think this stunned the major, and the sergeant major spoke up, "Specialist you get that red tape off this weapon and learn its serial number." It was extremely funny, but not a soldier broke a smile.

Soon the major stopped and checked me over. I was twenty and didn't shave. I tried to grow a mustache to look a little older. The sergeant major stopped in front of me and said, "One thing I can't stand is to see some boy try to grow a mustache."

He was waiting for a reply. I said, "Sergeant Major, with all due respect, if I am a boy, send my ass home." He paused for a moment, and I thought I was in serious trouble. The sergeant major turned and muttered, "Carry on, soldier."

I believe in every war this country fought, GIs have adopted dogs. We were no exception, although dogs were illegal. The company commander turned a blind eye to dogs and let us keep them in and near our barracks. Dogs were good for smelling someone who didn't belong near your hooch at night. Also, they alerted when rockets were inbound.

We had two dogs in our hooch or at least in our hooch area. The most famous was named Shaky. Some called him Tri-Pod because he only had three legs. I asked how he lost his leg and was told he had been run over while lying in the road. I have no clue if that was true or not.

Shakey was part hound and part bird dog. He had a tan-and-white fur and was a tall dog. Poor Shakey was sometimes seen up at the club where his water bowl was filled by soldiers leaving the club with beer. I've seen that poor dog drunk and not able to walk. Poor thing, but the next day he had shook it off and was up and around.

The second dog that stayed with us was named "Mr." He was a short whitish dog with short fur. While Shaky was friendly, Mr. was a grump. If you petted Mr., he would allow you to pet him for a short period of time before he snapped at you or bit you. When we received a new barracks mate, we always told them that Mr. loved to be petted and cuddled. The whole barracks would erupt in a huge roar of laughter as Mr. would bite the fire out of them. Yes our dogs had shots given to them on the sly. The medics would tell us when the veterinarians were coming to confiscate dogs. We had at least a day's notice where we would have Mommasons take the dogs home and care for them and bring them back. We warned Mommason that if she ate the dog, we would "cockadile" you (kill you). It was a joke we picked at with our Mommasons. Vietnamese have an appetite for dog meat. We didn't want that to be our dogs. After the veterinary sweep, our dogs would come back home and life would go on as usual.

If the Bien Hoa counter-battery radar picked up a missile launch, we would have about three seconds to react. The siren would go off, and everyone scrambled for cover. Bien Hoa took many 107mm and 122mm rocket attacks. The Viet Cong used the area north of the base as their staging area for rocket attacks. They would use slabs of banana tree bark or some other form of wooden launcher to place the rocket. They used the antenna lights to aim the rockets, so those lights were normally turned off. Interior lights were held to a minimum so as to keep accurate aiming down to a minimum. The antennae lights near Lassiter field were usually turned off, except for helicopter landings.

When rockets were fired, they made a sparkle tail like a smaller fireworks rocket kids play with at night or you see at a fireworks show. The rockets were a mile or so away when they went up and the dogs would bark wildly. I was never sure if they actually heard the "whoosh" of the rockets going up or reacted to the radar because either way, after the dogs reacted, you had seconds to make a move. If you couldn't make the bunker, you rolled under a bunk and pulled your mattress down on top of you. The dogs were always with us and never wandered away. They were an integral part of our band of brothers.

In December 1968, we were visited by the Ho Nai orphanage. They came to put on a little show for us. Our club was crammed with GIs watching the boys put on a sword-fighting dance. The girls did a ribbon dance, and they sang traditional Vietnamese songs. They were so cute, and all of us fell in love with them.

Stan S. and I took two little girls to dinner. We waited on them and carried their plates to our table. It was during this meal that we decided we wanted to help at the orphanage when they called on volunteers.

The nuns rounded up all the kids after the dinner, and they climbed aboard deuce and half trucks for their journey back home.

Chapter 9

THE WAR IN VIETNAM
1968 TO 1969

After five years of war, the VC and NVA continued to operate in South Vietnam, owning the night. They continued to infiltrate numerous troops into the south via the Ho Chi Minh Trail. The 1954 agreements between South Vietnam and North Vietnam were totally ignored by the North Vietnamese. Moreover, the TET offensive of 1968 had brought about the Paris peace talks. By 1969, some experts had suggested the United States should build border barriers and frontier protection along the DMZ and along the border between South Vietnam, Laos, and Cambodia.

Some ideas suggested electronic barriers or the manning of numerous outposts with land patrolling and electronic surveillance measures along the border, similar to what we had built in Korea. The bottom line is the vast frontier and jungle terrain did not lend itself to the development of any logical method to stop communist infiltration into the South (An Appropriate Response, by Col. George M. Shuffer Jr., US Army, December 1969, page 95).

Guard duty came around at least once or twice a week. We would meet at the engineer unit's command post area, located next to their sheltered theater. During guard mount, a lieutenant or captain would give us a briefing. Usually he was spitting back at us, verbatim, the intelligence report we had written the day before. Because of the sensitive nature of our job, we never let on to any outsiders what we really did at the 175th. The fact that we were the primary analytical intelligence unit in Vietnam was not the type of information we wanted out on the open market. Moreover, there was a $300 bounty on all intelligence personnel dead or alive in Vietnam.

More important, our operations building (the new building) was located within three hundred yards of the northern perimeter. It was painted a bright white paint scheme and stuck out against the brown and red sand and mud like a sore thumb. Rumor control had stated that if the enemy penetrated the perimeter, and if our building was going to be taken, the two fire support bases near us would turn their guns on our ops area and flatten and destroy everything, including us. The rumor also stated that we had a military police unit attached to our company as a means of shooting us before the enemy got to us. This was not a good feeling. After the guard mount briefing, we were loaded on to deuce and half trucks and ferried out to the perimeter.

Our bunker, built along the perimeter of the base, was built by pushing up dirt around a wooden shell built with 8 × 8 timbers. The roof had approximately three to four levels of sandbags to protect us from most rocket and mortar attacks. It was difficult for an anti-tank round to penetrate the bunkers. They were so well built that during the TET offensive of 1968, the VC used them as their last stand against our own helicopters and artillery. Believe it or not, our own bunkers proved to be a very difficult structure for our own forces to destroy. As a sidelight, when the ammunition dump at Bien Hoa was destroyed in 1968, the roof of these bunkers raised three feet in the air and came crashing back down in place.

Our company was responsible for eight bunkers that stretched from the fire support base to an L-shape in the northern perimeter fence line. Each bunker had three troops assigned to it. Inside the bunker, there were three fighting slits, built like a bay window. Each bunker had two five-eighths-inch plywood bunks built into it. These sleeping areas were never used by the troops because of little green viper snakes, rats, and spiders that lurked there. Everyone took their own cot to the bunker and the two off-duty soldiers would sleep outside, just behind the bunker. Because of the heavy dew, you would pull your poncho over your head before going to sleep. Additionally, this would also help keep mosquitoes from eating you alive, and sometimes even that didn't work.

In the center of the bunker was a stool. This is where the guard would spend his two-hour shift while the other two would sleep for four hours each. Each person would be equipped with his M-14 rifle. I carried eleven clips of ammo, plus we were given eight hand-grenades. The hand-grenade pins and handles were wrapped with black friction tape to keep us from blowing ourselves up. Additionally, one of the three of us would volunteer to be the grenadier and would be issued an

M-79 grenade launcher and one case of 40mm grenades. A second person would volunteer to carry the M-60 machine gun and approximately 1000 rounds of belted 7.62mm ammo. All of this firepower and ammunition would give us approximately ten minutes of fighting capability.

The bunkers were positioned about eighty to one hundred yards apart and were protected by five strands of barbwire. Out in front of the bunker I would set up five claymore mines and would check the lines to the two fifty-five-gallon drums of foo-gas (a mixture of jellied gasoline). The foo-gas was an idea designed by Air Force security police personnel and copied by the army all over Vietnam. Also, our perimeter was protected by booby traps and trip flares set by security police personnel. Approximately 500 yards apart were fifty-foot tall watchtowers. In the towers, two men would take turns manning a starlight scope all night. The starlight scope allowed you to see enemy movement and zoom it up close. Each tower was equipped with an M-60 machine gun, and each member carried his M-14 rifle. Behind each bunker sector was a circular pit built from sandbags; this was called the "mortar pit." The mortar men would only man the pit during attacks.

This would provide us with some direct artillery support and illumination support.

Some of our bunkers were located directly in front of the eight-inch howitzers and 175mm guns. I believe it was on two or three occasions I pulled guard duty here that I lost a little hearing. The concussion from the gun firing would cause your head to shrink and swell with each shot. It's pretty interesting to watch an eight-inch shell fly over your head and fly out sixteen miles to "touch someone." You can actually watch the shells fly away. The fire support bases (FSBs) were equipped with shells filled with flechette (razor blades) and were set up to provide a "killing fire" or "kill box" in front of the northern perimeter of the base. This is one reason Charlie (Viet Cong and North Vietnamese Regulars) decided to come through the city of Bien Hoa, south of the base near the airfield, rather than attempt a frontal assault against the northern perimeter.

Security was enhanced by the reduction of foliage. Agent Orange (a defoliant) was sprayed on the perimeter by an army defoliant truck. In February of 1969, the truck was given to the Air Force and the perimeter grass was beginning to grow tall again. According to Air Force records, a new 207–69 operations plan placed responsibility of defoliation on the 3rd Civil Engineering Squadron belonging to the 3rd Tactical Fighter Wing. Spraying was important because the VC had built numerous "spider holes" outside the fence of the northern perimeter (History of the 3rd Tactical Fighter Wing, 31 March 1969).

During the 1968 TET Offensive, our unit had captured a dozen VC caught in a crossfire and trapped in spider holes. A spider hole was a hole just large enough for a body to drop straight down into the hole and roll under an underground shelf. This protected the VC from artillery and machine gun fire while allowing them to be within range of our perimeter with their anti-tank weapons and rifles. The only way to ferret them out was to use a helicopter and hover over the hole and drop hand grenades into the hole. TET is the Vietnamese New Year and marks the beginning of the year of the next animal. TET of 1969 was the year of the rooster. February of 1969 was going to be a very lively event in the Bien Hoa–Long Binh area.

I was instructed to always assume the VC, or NVA, were near at night. However, there was no free fire zone without consent from the operations center. Sometimes our own Special Forces were outside the wire, crawling in the grass looking for bad guys. We did not want to accidentally kill our own men.

When I moved into the Order of Battle section, I was mentored by several older married men. I think the oldest was twenty-three. He had a funny personality, pleasant, and always had some sort of proverbial wisdom. "Luikart, let me warn you about something: don't marry a girl that has snakes in her head." That is a great proverb for younger men to adhere to.

Our intelligence section sifted through mounds of captured documents, prisoner-of-war interrogations, and daily reports of contacts with the enemy in III and IV Corps areas. I learned how to sift quickly, looking for key phrases, words, or "also known as" (AKA), information. Our AKA file was 3 × 5 cards with the key word at the top, and alphanumerically filed. Our file stayed on our desk and was two rows of cards in a long tray, about three feet long. We had AKA information on everything tied to the war—every unit, commander's name, location, type weapons, or any item used by the enemy. We had all the AKA information at our fingertips. If an analyst asked us about "Commander P20," we could find that information in seconds.

I also kept INTREPs, or intelligence reports, from II Field Force and all the Divisions in the III and IV Corps area. I also kept a file on other top-secret files created by Special Forces. (Phoenix Program) My job was to assist our Texta analysts in developing their signals structure of enemy units. I was able to prove, through collateral intelligence, the location of a unit, a unit move, large buildup, cache, or anything the analyst was looking for. We also assisted the code breakers with their manuscripts they were developing in Vietnamese. Many times, the VC used codes for everything. My AKA file was probably the best in Vietnam; made of old-school cards, it was very effective.

We kept unit strength and logistics trails. We could follow large shipments from North Vietnam all the way down to the Elephant's Ear, Dog's Face, or Parrot's Beak areas. Following these movements as best we could would tell us which unit was rebuilding its strength and logistics for a possible attack. We had cards developed for each enemy division, regiment, and battalion in our area of responsibility. This included all the enemy combat engineer battalions that planted bombs and conducted harassing attacks against local US and ARVN military facilities. We kept strength, location, training, weapons and equipment, and commanding officer information on each unit we followed. I knew the enemy better than I knew our own forces' capabilities.

One of the most primitive, yet effective, tools was the daily "pinning" of all the radio hits our aircraft picked up in III and IV Corps. These were called "aerial radio direction finding" (ARDF) files that listed the location of every enemy radio in use for the day. Monday's pins might be black, Tuesday's red, and perhaps on Wednesday, I used yellow pins.

I would sit down at a large map of the III and IV Corps area and pin each radio hit for the day. It took several hours to pin well over three hundred hits. After the map was pinned, the senior leaders of each section would meet with the operations officer, and they would discuss the mass of pins on the map. It was very easy to spot that one radio or radios that were suddenly moved away from the normal location. Using this simple pin map, our analysts started looking for activity in War Zone C that was usually quiet. The pin map probably gave away the movement of an enemy division forward operating base. We actually could watch the enemy come toward us. It was a surreal job, knowing you were the target of a division-sized Viet Cong force.

Since it took days and weeks for them to establish themselves, we had time to counter their move and strike their troops first. All this was based on very good analytical work, message decoding, and language experts, radio communications experts, and good intelligence analysts, and finally, that one, very important, super pinned map. Sometimes the simplest tool gets the job done.

Chapter 10

VC/NVA MOVEMENTS IN OCTOBER 1968 THROUGH FEBRUARY 1969

I t has always been my assessment that the North Vietnamese leadership ordered Viet Cong–led infantry divisions to lead the attacks in the 1968 TET Offensive. During this offensive, thousands of VC infantry division casualties weakened traditional VC units. In addition, one of North Vietnam's, Senior General Nguyen Chi Thanh, was killed in Hanoi on 6 July, 1967. Supposedly died of a heart attack. He was the primary adviser to the South Vietnamese communists and now he was gone. The vacuum was filled by General Giap, the North Vietnamese Supreme General. (The History 1946-1975 Vietnam at War, Lt Gen Phillip B. Davidson, USA Ret., page 463)

A Viet Cong guerrilla fighter would be conscripted into a local VC infantry battalion. These local battalions were sapper units, setting traps and carrying out special operations. After several years of service, a guerrilla fighter would be promoted to sergeant. He was given a choice of being promoted into a VC division, or stay in the guerrilla unit. If he wanted the rank and would go to the VC Divisions he would receive, more pay, and more food for his family. After the 1968 TET Offensive and the TET of 1969 (called the mini TET), VC Divisions were back filled with North Vietnamese Army Regulars. This caused big problems for Viet Cong divisions and regiments. Fist fights occurred over women between the two camps. When I say women, I mean the South Vietnamese soldiers' wives, daughters, or girlfriends. North Vietnamese soldiers were not used to South Vietnamese customs, and it caused headaches for their leadership. Even today, all these years later, there is within Vietnam a split between North and South Vietnamese.

During October 15 and November 15, 1968, I spent most of the night in a bunker during heavy rocket attacks on Bien Hoa Army and Air Force Base. On both those dates, nationwide antiwar demonstrations occurred in the United States. This was so disturbing to those of us in Vietnam that one of my buddies wrote a letter to several newspapers back in the States. In this letter, he asked that the *Stars and Stripes* be changed to a *Field of Red* (for the blood of American soldiers who had died for freedom) with a very large yellow chicken in the center representing the American people. The antiwar demonstrations were having a very significant effect on the fighting men in Vietnam.

After the TET offensive in 1968, the big question on all the experts' minds was who was really winning—the enemy or us. The 1968 bombings of Hanoi led to Paris peace talks. As soon as the North Vietnamese agreed to the peace talks, Johnson stopped the bombing. I was dumbfounded. We were irritated because for us, the war had not changed and neither had the rocket attacks on our base. There was a change of administration in the White House, Nixon for Johnson and a change of command in Vietnam. General Creighton Abrams replaced General William C. Westmoreland. Nixon's advisers were asking him to take a hard line against the North Vietnamese communists, Nixon developed a strategy of "Vietnamization" to extricate ourselves out of the country. Meanwhile, General Abrams designed the strategy of attacking the COSVN (Communist Organization of South Vietnam) and NLF (National Liberation Front of Vietnam) headquarters, trying to kill NVA General Giap. General Abrams wanted ground bomb damage assessment to be conducted by the infantry immediately after B-52 strikes. This was costly and very hazardous duty for those grunts tasked to carry out this order.

It may have been coincidental, but those of us in Vietnam listening to the news or reading a *Stars and Stripes* felt very strongly that collusion occurred between the communist attacks in South Vietnam and the antiwar sympathizer demonstrations in the United States. Some ministers can attest to the fact that many churches in the United States were collecting and storing medical supplies, bandages, and drugs to be shipped to the VC and NVA via a friendly flagged ship. Merchant ships flying a recognizable supposed ally flag would slip into Phnom Penh, formerly called Sihanoukville, Cambodia, and unload supplies for the enemy. Those supplies would be trucked northeast toward the Parrot's Beak and into the Viet Cong and North Vietnam's logistics supply areas.

The year 1969 proved to be the second bloodiest year of the war, even if it was the least talked-about phase of the war. More than nine hundred Americans were killed each month during 1969.

You must remember that men who had fought in World War II were leading our ground forces. Attrition warfare was a common practice, but not very popular. Combat casualties were considered a price that had to be paid to close and kill the enemy. Moreover, antiwar demonstrations and speeches gave the enemy the opinion that most Americans were against the war. General Lewis W. Walt complained that the news media was not reporting the real war to viewer's back home. The TV coverage was taking small, remote, daylight engagements and making a big deal out of them while most of the fighting was done at night. General Walt hit the nail on the head. Television depictions of battles were skewed to make headlines rather than tell the truth about the engagements conducted by the grunts in Vietnam.

During 1969 and early 1970, our intelligence unit attempted to locate and kill General Giap in the COSVN area between the Fish Hook, a bend in the river near An Loc, and the Dog's Head, a geographical area along the Cambodian border. Our unit would study the COSVN movement patterns and attempt to predict their next move. Every week we developed a list of potential targets that were forwarded to the II Field Force Commander (a three-star general). His staff would incorporate all the potential targeted areas and then choose the targets to be bombed. Within hours, B-52s from Guam would be on their way to shake the jungle. I have seen B-52 strikes from less than ten miles away; it feels like an earthquake, and the rumble sounds like thunder in the mountains. We were not successful, but according to General Giap's own book. We came close to killing him more than once.

Interestingly, Nixon's advisers suggested some form of "selective bombing" in North Vietnam. Targets chosen were stockpiles of ammunition, weapons, and petroleum storage areas recently installed just north of the DMZ. In the south, more than 575 tactical air sorties, about one hundred more than usual, struck VC and NVA positions. B-52s carried out ten strikes against enemy base camps, weapons positions, and storage areas supporting the three divisions attacking Long Binh and Bien Hoa. One of these attacks occurred near Bien Hoa in War Zone D and was quite visible from our location. The earth shook, and the attack could be seen and heard more than fifteen miles away (History of the 3rd TFW, Jan–March 1969).

During January and February 1969, B-52s attacked VC and NVA strongholds with more than two million pounds of bombs in the Parrot's Beak area, near the Cambodian border. Some of these attacks were targets I had forwarded to the II Field Force commander as candidates for ARC LIGHT strikes. The areas were historically the 9th VC Division area of operations near the Parrot's Beak (*New York Times*, 19 Feb 1969).

Additionally, we chose local targets to be attacked with H & I (Harass and Interdict) artillery. When we found a significant enemy unit that appeared to be stationary, we would write down the coordinates, take them to the Tactical Operations Center (TOC), and turn them over to their operations sergeant. At the TOC, we would verify that the enemy unit was located in a free fire zone and that no friendly operations were in the area. Immediately after verification, the fire-support bases would open up with their eight-inch guns or 175mm howitzers, or both. These guns could throw a shell sixteen miles at a target and hit the target with pretty good accuracy. I often wondered how many people were killed on the other end because our intelligence section chose them to receive the artillery barrage.

Chapter 11

THE FORGOTTEN BATTLE– MINI TET OF FEBRUARY 1969

I n February 1969, I witnessed a very large battle for the control of Bien Hoa Army and Air Base. I had just turned twenty-one years old on February 1st and had been in the country only six months. It was about this time I quickly learned to tell the difference between outgoing artillery fire from fire support bases and incoming 122mm and 107mm rockets. Moreover, I learned the difference between incoming rockets, which are very inaccurate, and incoming mortars, which are very accurate.

The Mini-TET Offensive of February 1969, or as some people call it the "Post TET Offensive," cost about 250 American lives and more than 3,000 Viet Cong lives. The VC attacks did not make any sense at all, except that the North Vietnamese government ordered another offensive be conducted with

VC units. During the latter part of 1968, and early 1969, many of the VC divisions were starving to death and were complaining to their higher headquarters that their men were eating grass and banana leaves. This absurd attack order, from the enemy higher headquarters, further proves my point. This attack further weakened the traditional VC divisions, and North Vietnamese were used to back fill the units after the battle. By the end of our involvement in Vietnam, NVA regulars were staffing traditional VC leadership positions.

The North Vietnamese communists ordered the 5th VC division to attack Bien Hoa and Long Binh. The goal of these attacks was to overrun the American bases at Long Binh and Bien Hoa and feast on the US soldier's "rations." According to Special Forces personnel who recovered weapons off the battlefield, many of the communist dead had "P38" can openers on chains around their necks. Obviously they were serious about eating our rations. Throughout January and February of 1969, the 5th VC division relocated from Cambodia to the southern part of War Zone D, approximately thirty kilometers (eighteen miles) northeast of Bien Hoa Air Base. On 15 February, elements of the division moved to forward positions to the north and east of Bien Hoa Air Base. As a side note, in 1968, Company D of the 151st Regiment, Indiana Army National Guard was activated for service with the II Field Force. These men were used in very small seven-man teams, perhaps smaller, but usually seven men. They were inserted in the path or near suspected enemy concentrations. Basically, their mission was to collect information on the approximate size, location, and direction of movement of enemy columns. They also reported on types of weapons and approximate numbers. These intelligence reports, used with the radio interceptions we received, helped paint the picture of what enemy intentions were.

In early 1969, prior to the TET Holiday, Intelligence reports indicated there was a large and general movement of forces southward from the Cambodian border areas located northwest and north of Saigon. A meeting of all the top US Commanders was called. Colonel Patton, commander of the 11th Armored Cav Regiment, explained he felt the base would be hit by a regimental-sized enemy unit and that *Long Binh* was the primary target because of its logistical supply caches. While Bien Hoa had a very important air base, the VC were interested in overrunning

Long Binh. He pointed out that the enemy felt that Long Binh was "lightly defended." One side of its main perimeter ran along Highway Route 1 and was considered a weak point. Patton used intelligence reporting from the 175th RRC as his basis for substantiating his assessment. Perhaps they would take a provincial capital, any provincial capital would do, declare a new government in South Vietnam and sue for peace that removed us from the country. That was their deep underlying motive.

Regardless of their motive for attack, our intelligence section knew the enemy was coming at us. The 5th VC division moved east of Long Binh, into the War Zone D area. The 1st NVA moved north along highway 13, apparently to keep that corridor open. The 7th NVA division moved down highway 13 out of the Fishhook area into the Michelin rubber plantation. The 7th NVA would replace the 1st NVA division after it was hit hard and was retreating back toward the COSVN area and on into Cambodia. The 9th VC division moved southeast of Tay Ninh City out of the Parrot's Beak area and was operating between Bien Hoa and Tay Ninh City, a distance of only seventy miles from Saigon.

On one night prior to the February attack, I was assigned as a tower guard. Tower guards pulled a twenty-four-hour shift, two hours on and two hours off during the night, and one guard staying awake in the tower all day the next day. During the night, I spotted about fifty enemy troops moving through a local rubber tree plantation approximately 500 yards away. They were moving from my left to my right. It may have been a test to see if we were able to engage them or see their movement. That night I was using a starlight scope. The starlight scope was large and heavy, but allowed you to see the night as daylight with a green-colored tint. On that occasion, the TOC scrambled a helicopter gunship that engaged the enemy and killed several of them. You had to be careful shooting at movement in front of your bunker because US Special Forces and Vietnamese marines would spend many nights moving about outside the perimeter looking for VC/NVA spies and forward observers. Indiscriminately shooting at someone outside the wire could mean killing one of your own troops!

Throughout the week, prior to 23 February, the number of contacts with the enemy within eighteen miles of the base was light, and the size of the enemy units were mainly squad size or smaller. Agent reports and prisoner-of-war inter-rogations confirmed that a pending offensive was planned to begin on or immediately after the 1969 TET holidays.

What was fascinating about the movement of the 5th VC division into an area as close as ten miles north and east of Bien Hoa was that my intelligence collateral map and signals intelligence map locations married up, showing that the 5th was on the move. Usually a big division like that sends out its "advanced headquarters" or scouts and sets up rudimentary headquarters, waiting on the arrival of the main division. Then when the headquarters' elements start moving, our bases were under surveillance from the enemy from on top of a small hill near Bien Hoa. Actually, it was a Buddhist temple location, so it was off limits to shelling. Then the rear guard headquarters ele-ment would show up, showing about how long the division was, physically, in the area of opera-tion. It was strung out for miles. Every intelligence unit used the long range reconnaissance patrol (LRRP) reports. The US IIFFV Commander used them as his "eyes and ears" in the field. I have the highest respect for these men. It is why I was upset when the US Army used the black beret as their formal hat because the Black Beret was worn by LRRPs in Vietnam.

As early as 17 February, intelligence indicated that the weekend of 23 February was a critical period throughout all of Vietnam. The security at Bien Hoa was beefed up and augmentation forces were put on alert. Bien Hoa had 245 security police augmented by sixty-five Air Force Reserve security police trained in crew-served weapons (106mm recoilless rifles); fifty-three sentry dogs, and 145 Air Force augmenters who could be called on if necessary. Stationed at Bien Hoa was the 145th Aviation Battalion, who had sixty fighting positions in the integrated portion of the southern perimeter, and had two helicopter firefly teams, one light-ship, and two gunships available. Additionally, the 11th Armored Cavalry Regiment, 23rd ARVN Defense Force Group, and the 57th ARVN regional forces and the 5th Republic of Vietnam marines, and Army and Air Force K-9 units, using German Shepherd dogs, provided additional security.

The northern perimeter was guarded by elements of the US Army Engineer Battalion and the 175th Radio Research Company. The 11th Armored Cav provided armored assistance; three Sheridan tanks and six Armored Personnel Carriers (APC's). The 44th Artillery Regiment furnished two Vulcan APCs. One APC I distinctly noticed was a M113 with quad 50s mounted on top. I later learned through historical records that this was an Air Force security police–designed vehicle.

By 19 February 1969, our intelligence section knew we were going to be attacked sometime on 22 or 23 February. Our assessment stated the Viet Cong and North Vietnamese would attempt a series of simultaneous assaults on various province capitals in order to influence the Paris talks and to attempt to capture a province capital in order to bring a quicker closure to the campaign. Moreover, some of the analysts I worked with felt that the VC and NVA had set up their military regions (MR) like spokes in a wheel, with Saigon as the hub and all other MRs spiking out from it. This allowed the VC and NVA units to always concentrate their efforts toward the capital city, Saigon.

On 20 February, a large number of enemy soldiers were killed in Binh Duong Province, eighteen miles northwest of Saigon. This area was believed to be the area of interest of VC and NVA forces for conducting their attacks against South Vietnamese and US forces. Tay Ninh City was very close to the Parrot's Beak, and Long Binh and Bien Hoa were the two largest military bases within easy striking distance of enemy forces camped in Cambodia.

Bien Hoa was a crowded base with about 17,000 personnel and 350 aircraft, not counting the helicopters owned by the army. More than 70,000 air movements monthly meant the base was the busiest airport in the world. Fuel consumption was estimated at 8,000 gallons per twenty-four hours (3rd Tactical Fighter Wing SPOT Intelligence report, 1969).

COSVN, or the North Vietnamese, could not ignore the importance of Long Binh and Bien Hoa. These were large complexes, staffed by troops considered to be rear area forces and not combat soldiers. The communists considered these complexes as easy targets to attack and overrun.

On 21 February 1969, enemy activity throughout Vietnam died down to a whimper. From a total of eighty-nine countrywide incidents a day to only fourteen on Wednesday and four on Thursday, just prior to the attack on our base. This was a big indicator that something big was going to happen.

The level of US activity of "bomb and sweep with the infantry" resulted in more than 197 US soldiers killed during the week. It wasn't much of a strategy, but General Abrams was testing out new methods of engaging the enemy. The ARC LIGHT strikes would hit suspected VC or NVA command centers, and the infantry would sweep through to do a ground bomb damage assessment (BDA) and attempt to capture or kill the VC and NVA headquarters personnel.

On 21 February, the United States urged the North Vietnamese and Viet Cong to seek "common ground" for negotiations at the Paris peace talks. During that meeting, the South Vietnamese delegation called for an exchange of prisoners of war, but the North Vietnamese and VC government representatives remained silent on that point. The peace talks weren't going anywhere.

Interestingly, on 22 February 1969, five leaders of United States church organizations demanded that Nixon give them a "clear statement of American intentions in Vietnam." This was the typical behavior of US church leaders and other antiwar dissidents prior to a large enemy offensive in Vietnam. Antiwar activists appeared to step up their rhetoric one or two days prior to a countrywide communist offensive. The belief that collusion between these antiwar activists and North Vietnamese communists was real, and posed a counterintelligence threat to the war effort.

The Army and Air base at Bien Hoa was attacked on the 23 and 26 February 1969. First attack attempted to penetrate the Air Base. The second attack attempted to penetrate the US Army front gate. The sprawling army base was attached to the airbase and covered most of the area north of the air strip.

On 23 February, at 2:10 a.m., guard tower number 10 reported incoming rounds from the east and northeast, about three miles from the base. These rounds were 107mm rockets that leave a distinct golden shower of sparkles as they go up into the sky. The warning siren was sounded, and I hit the floor and rolled under the bunk. You only had three to nine seconds to react. Because I felt we were going to be hit that night, I went to bed fully dressed with my boots laced. I had my helmet, rifle, and flak vest in bed with me. At 2:14 a.m. a second volley of rockets was reported incoming (3rd Tactical Wing After-Action Reports for February 1969).

Immediately, each hooch went into a self-protection mode. Instead of heading to a covered bunker, we made our way to either end of the hooch and spread out, watching the open area between the hooches for any kind of hostile fire. We knew that VC Sappers, enemy commandos, were very capable of penetrating the base, and until the perimeter was augmented, there would be gaps between bunkers.

Most of Bien Hoa City and the base lost all power as a result of impacts, or someone turned off the power to our area of the base. It was pitch black. The augmentation guard had been called to report to the orderly room when this second volley hit. The darkened base became hauntingly scary as we were ordered to take up fighting positions within our own company area. At 2:20 a.m., additional incoming rounds were reported. The number of rounds hitting our base created a problem with an accurate count; the barrage was the worst I had ever encountered in Vietnam, and I had encountered quite a few attacks.

On the day of the attack when the augmentation guard was called out, the bunker I entered had a 106mm recoilless rifle, mounted on a jeep, on my right side and a M113 armored personnel carrier, with the quad 50 caliber machine guns, parked on my left side. With this amount of firepower within spitting distance from me, with me in the middle, I felt like a target. I went back outside, I felt safer.

At 2:50 a.m. tower number 6 on the south perimeter, near the Air Base, reported that it was receiving small arms fire from the direction of "Turkey Row," a road lined with shacks that runs parallel to the perimeter and part of Bien Hoa City. This was an old VC trick; they would attack the base perimeter using civilian homes built against the perimeter fence as cover. Most of these houses belonged to ARVN Air Force Officers that built as close to the base as possible.

Tower number 8 also received fire from Turkey Row. All units on the southern perimeter were ordered by the Air Force security police to open fire on the incoming enemy gun fire. One Sherman tank and one APC were moved up and opened fire. Security police reaction forces were deployed behind tower number 8 as well as at sentry dog post number 1 and in the vicinity of base gate number 3.

Tower number 6 and tower number 8 reported observing the enemy establishing two mortar positions and one machine gun position along Turkey Row. US Army helicopters were on scene in the area. The APC vehicle responded to the vicinity of the tower number 8 and opened fire on the suspected enemy locations. All these positions were eliminated, meaning all the enemy in these locations were killed. Seven individuals were observed by tower number 8 crossing Turkey Row toward the base perimeter, but suppressive fire by base security police diverted them, and they were forced back to their original positions inside the civilian houses in Turkey Row (3rd Tactical Wing After-Action Reports, February 1969).

During this time frame, our augmentation guard was ordered to go into the bunkers along the northern perimeter as soon as possible. In the early morning pitch-black environment, our twenty-man team climbed into two deuce and halfs and moved at a snail's pace toward the northern perimeter. When we approached the bunkers, not much was said by anyone. Everyone was awake and alert, and all weapons were locked and loaded. Augmentation of the bunkers meant that some of us would have to remain outside and dig foxholes into the perimeter berm rather than go inside the crowded bunker. I dug a foxhole into the berm and setup my ammo for easy reloading. I had no plan for a retreat or a place to run to; as a matter of fact, I had made a commitment to stay and fight until capture. Under my armpit was a pistol intended to end things quickly if necessary, or in other words, it was there to enable me to commit suicide if necessary to avoid capture. At 3:45 a.m. the battle quieted and ceased.

At 4:30 a.m., security supervisors checked their areas and reported incoming rounds over the radio. The siren was sounded. A number of rounds impacted south of the base, probably into Bien Hoa City. At the same time, small-arms fire erupted again from Turkey Row (3rd Tactical Fighter After-Action Reports, February 1969).

During the early morning hours, each of us felt very uneasy because the fighting was coming from behind us. Our perimeter was quiet, except for the occasional rocket we observed sparkling skyward from the jungle along the Song Dong Nai river (Song means river in Vietnamese) to the north of us. All of these rounds would whoosh over our heads and impact the Army or Air Force base behind us. At this time, the northern perimeter was probably the safest place to be.

At 5:09 a.m., the 145th Aviation Battalion Operations Center reported incoming rounds and again the siren was sounded. Incoming B-40 (anti-tank rounds) were reported coming from the school building in Bien Hoa City, directly across from the base main gate. Small arms and automatic weapons fire continued until 6:28 a.m., when the 145th Aviation Battalion reported incoming rounds. This report, however, was a false alarm (3rd Tactical Fighter After-Action Reports, February 1969).

At 7:00 a.m., all firing ceased and the 23rd Defense Force Group made a sweep on Turkey Row between the main gate and gate number 3. At 7:50 hours, security alert "Condition Gray" was initiated. Elements of the 3rd Security Police Squadron swept the interior of the south perimeter with negative results (3rd Tactical Fighter After-Action Reports, February 1969).

Before dawn, elements of the 5th VC division fired more than fifty-four rockets into Bien Hoa Army and Air Force Base. These were identified as 107mm rockets (3rd Tactical Fighter After-Action Reports, February 1969).

I doubt anyone had an accurate count of the number of rockets, and this estimate was based on those that the Air Force counted and not what had hit us on the Army side. I estimated the count at more than seventy before the barrage ended when I lost count. The 107mm rockets, being very inaccurate, caused no injuries or deaths, but pinned down the base while a ground force attempted to penetrate the base perimeter. The firefight on the south perimeter, from direction of Bien Hoa City, was directed at the weakest area of the base. Historically, South Vietnamese military families would build their homes against the perimeter fence, next to where they worked on the base. A year earlier, during the 1968 TET offensive, the VC and NVA forces penetrated the Long Binh, Bien Hoa, and Ton Son Nhut bases by going through civilian housing. This trick would be used by communist forces in Colombia in the 1980's. Using civilians and their homes as a shield against friendly forces using artillery, and air attacks, became a part of their world wide play book. In 1987, I observed the same type of conditions at numerous Thai bases I visited in Thailand.

We remained in place for the next five days. Meals on wheels had a new meaning. We were brought a pretty good box lunch every day and rotated in for a hot meal once a day, but we spent all night on the perimeter. Enemy movement was reported every night outside our perimeter. Additionally, ARVN and US Special Forces would set up listening posts in front of our positions at night. We had a killing zone of about one-mile that had been defoliated by aerial spray. Agent Orange sure made us feel safer back then, regardless of its long-range effect on some us today. Pushing the jungle back one mile gave us plenty of time to react to a large attack. It was the snipers and sappers we feared the most.

While on the perimeter, we set up five claymore mines. Behind each claymore, we placed several sandbags. The back blast was as deadly as the frontal blast. We were instructed to always duck down below the parapet if we had to set off the mines. We also checked our mines regularly to make sure the enemy did not turn one toward our bunker. This was a trick they used countrywide. There were trip flares set up and maintained by Air Force security forces. These were checked regularly by the Air Force SF troops.

Bien Hoa had five fences between the outside world and the bunkers. Beyond the fences was a small plantation of rubber trees, a village, and the Song Dong Nai. On occasions, fire fights would occur on the Song Dong Nai between enemy forces and US Navy patrol boats. It was interesting to watch the firefight occur and made you realize the enemy was not far from your position.

I watched AC-47 gunships working over Long Binh on the nights of 23 and 24 February 1969. Spooky or "Puff the Magic Dragon," as we called them, were back breakers. Now, I don't know a lot about the specifics of an AC-47 except what I observed. When their "electronic" machine guns — Gatling guns — fired at the ground, a continuous red ribbon flowed from the aircraft to the ground like someone was spraying a water hose filled with red water. Whoever was on the ground was receiving an overwhelming number of bullets.

On 24 February 1969, an attack occurred against Long Binh, only seven miles away. During this attack, the perimeter of the base was about to be penetrated when the Air Force dispatched a "Puff the Magic Dragon." We knew that the attack was a bust because they killed about 130 VC in the wire. I believe these VC were from the 274th VC regiment, 5th VC division.

During the attack, a Magic Dragon was hit by heavy ground fire and caused a flare to ignite inside the aircraft. According to what I understand,

A1C John Levitow was briefly knocked out by the explosion. When he woke up, the floor of the aircraft was covered with his own blood. Sergeant Levitow had forty-plus shrapnel wounds in his back. Unable to stand on the slippery surface bloody, he crawled over to an armed flare, picked it up, crawled to an open hatch and threw it out of the aircraft. His actions saved the plane and crew. Immediately after the flare left the aircraft it exploded, burning his face and arms.

For this action he received the Congressional Medal of Honor. Only two Medals of Honor have been presented to Air Force enlisted men for their actions during the Vietnam War. It didn't dawn on me that Levitow and I had participated in the same battle until I read his account in the museum at Squadron Officer School in 1986.

Unfortunately, except for the battle at Hamburger Hill that took place in May of 1969 between the 101st Airborne Division and some 1000 North Vietnamese Regular soldiers, historians often forget about the Mini-TET offensive of 1969. During Hamburger Hill, some 84 Americans were killed, and more than 600 North Vietnamese Regulars were killed.

It was on 25 February that one of our unit members was killed on a routine mission to a local village. His name was SP5 Harold Douglas Biller from Silver Springs, Maryland. Doug's name is on 31W Line 43 on the Vietnam War Memorial in Washington D.C. Doug and Dave Reiser were on a supply mission from Nui Dat to a Special Forces camp in a nearby town to pick up new uniforms for his outfit. A general was coming to Nui Dat to inspect the men, and everyone had worn and ragged uniforms. Water was scant at Nui Dat, so picking up new uniforms seemed a smart idea. If the general had not scheduled the visit, perhaps Harold would be alive today. "Such is fate" in war. I agree.

Nui Dat, like many ASA units in Vietnam, was a small compound stuck out in the middle of nowhere, working detection equipment looking for the enemy. The 175th had dozens of these smaller radio research units, or detachments (email from Dave Reiser, 2017).

Harold was a SP5 and was the senior man. Dave Reiser was a SP4 and was going to be the door gunner in the truck. But Harold (Doug) decided he wanted to be the door gunner, and so having traded positions that's how they left the base at Nui Dat.

Harold carried the M79 grenade launcher with a grenade locked and loaded in the breach. He also carried a bandelaro of grenades with him. We were in the middle of the Mini Tet '69 offensive when the local MPs opened up the road to traffic. They were in the middle of an Aussie column of M113s. They were about a mile outside the gate when the VC command detonated two land mines. They believe the land mines were 120mm US artillery shells. Harold's grenade launcher or grenades went off, and he was thrown up out of his seat and on the tailgate of the truck. The blast almost amputated his leg. He was still alive, but bleeding to death. Dave was also hit with the blast and was dazed. Because a battle ensued and bullets were flying everywhere, Dave crawled into a ditch and took cover. The Aussies found six Viet Cong killed in a hidden bunker along the road. This was, unfortunately, typical. Local sapper battalions were always present.

They tried to secure Harold's leg with an M14 rifle that Harold was also toting with him. The M14 barrel was bent from the explosion. Dave, the driver, was seriously injured as well, with numerous scars and black eyes from the blast. Harold was loaded in a helicopter (called a Dust Off) to the closest medical facility, but he expired on the way. Dave, thinking he was okay, stayed behind. However, he was wounded severely and finally felt the wounds and was treated by the Aussies.(email from Dave Reiser, 2017).

I have not given the full account of this story, and there is more to tell, but I will leave that up to Dave to add to this and make this story more accurate.

On the night of 25 February, we rotated man-power onto the perimeter. I ended up sleeping in the intelligence section under the desk and worked a twenty-four-hour day. Early in the morning of 26 February, an enemy force of more than 300 men, probably the 275th VC Regiment, were observed off the east perimeter of Bien Hoa AFB. This Regiment moved into a natural draw running from the front gate area eastward toward Long Binh. I distinctly remember taking a photograph shortly after the battle of a little house where this VC unit murdered all the family members. I painted a house, similar to that dwelling, and is the front cover of this book.

I figure they were going to use this draw as an attack avenue to the gate. The front gate was attacked, and they attempted to breach the army base where I was located. Actually the tip off may have been from civilians fleeing the area after VC units began to pour into the hamlets of Tam Heip and Ho Nai. Heavy fighting ensued during the rest of the morning. About 6:00 a.m., we were ordered back to the northern perimeter where sporadic sniper fire was received on the base until 5:45 p.m.

During the day we would step out to watch the helicopters attack the VC trapped in the two hamlets. Stray bullets would ricochet around our heads after impacting the ground. We were not sure if it was sniper fire or just stray bullets from someone's gun less than 2000 feet away. Luckily this sporadic fire did not hit anyone.

The perimeter was not breached, but the estimated 100 to 300 VC successfully maneuvered to within 1,000 meters of Bien Hoa's army gate. We discussed perhaps the 174th VC regiment/5th VC division was to hit the northern perimeter where we were, but they never materialized. Perhaps they were lost, or just not in place for a full on frontal assault.

Friendly forces engaged this force in a heated firefight near the front gate. Later that day, Air Force F100s were called in to pound the VC positions that had dug into the civilian homes within the hamlets. Remember, the civilians had fled or were allowed to leave. In the early afternoon, the 3rd Tactical Fighter Wing's 531st TAC fighter squadron sent two F-100 aircraft up to attack VC elements at Tam Heip. Two F-100 "Ramrods" attacked a VC ground assault off the end of Bien Hoa Air Base. The two pilots were Major Joseph K. Brown and Lieutenant James M. Shea. According to 3TFW sources, the 275th VC regiment, 5th VC division, suffered more than 214 killed. The Special Forces figures put the number at approximately 296 killed. A picture of the aftermath is sitting in my office and shows the damage done to the cities by our attacks.

After the F-100s attacked, South Vietnamese A1 Skyraiders attacked with 750-pound and 1000-pound bombs. I had never had the opportunity to watch the Air Force at work at such close range to our positions, probably a mile and a half away. The F100s used a low angle attack and used four mk82hd bombs, four BLU-27 bombs, and 700 rounds of 20mm. I listened to the attack on the tactical radio and according to the radio chatter, the VC/NVA soldiers were caught in a small draw or ravine and more than two dozen were killed instantly by F100 20mm cannon fire.

Results to US forces were: killed in action—none; wounded in action—four; and missing in action—none. No enemy penetrated the base. Sapper penetration was not confirmed by after-action reports.

The fighting in the little hamlets of Tam Heip and Ho Nai forced numerous civilians to flee for their lives. According to some reports, ARVN Marines talked the remaining VC into giving up their hostages and surrendering. They gave up their hostages, but refused to surrender. After the air attacks, those that survived, and there wasn't many, told of the horrors of the napalm. The next day one of our unit members walked along the road near the southern perimeter and observed blackened and bloated bodies that appeared to die in running positions, lying in a military-style assault formation, but on their sides. It was a pretty sickening site, but his curiosity had gotten the better of him, and he paid the price for being nosy. He snapped a roll of film, and I got photocopies of the carnage.

During out-processing for home, US Army inspectors confiscated the photos and a piece of shrapnel I dug out of the ground, except for the one photo I keep on my desk, I had mailed that photo home to my parents. It didn't show any bodies, just the building blown to shreds by F100s and cobra gunships. It was also from this attack I acquired my 7.62 Russian "Short" (referring to the size of the cartridge) Mosin Nagant carbine picked up by Army Special Forces off the battlefield.

The result of the four rocket attacks between 23 February and 31 March 1969 was a destruction of property, supplies, and equipment, valued at over two million dollars. Bien Hoa continued to be a prime target throughout the war. In 1968, Bien Hoa received twice as many rocket rounds and mortar attacks than any other air base in all of South Vietnam. So many attacks occurred here that we kept our cameras set up on tripods every night trying to get that best "rocket hit" photo. I have a couple of colored slides showing a rocket hitting the base engineer theater mentioned earlier, and a picture of an F-100 aircraft burning up on the Air Force base.

During the Mini-TET of February 1969, more than 115 US installations were attacked throughout South Vietnam. At least three enemy divisions, possibly four, were operating in the area of Saigon—the 5th VC, 9th VC, 7th NVA, and 1st NVA divisions. During the first fifteen hours of the countrywide offensive, more than one hundred US soldiers were killed. Forty-eight hours later, the number climbed to two hundred Americans killed.

On the early morning of the 26 February VC Sappers attacked Chu Chi Army Base. They were warned of an impending attack and were prepared with additional guards sleeping on their CH 47 helicopters (Chinooks) and extra men in the bunkers. The augmentation guard was prepared to respond to any attack and plug gaps made by the enemy into the base. About 80 to 100 VC Commandos cut through 10 fences, slowly making their way through each fence using the darkness as their protection.

The moon was waxing "Gibbous" and provided about 50% of its illumination. The dates of 21 through 27 February for an all out assault country wide was not a mistake, or a hap hazard decision. These were the times when the moon was waxing and the crescent moonlight was used by the VC for night vision. We always called waxing and waning moon phases a "Viet Cong Moon."

After the VC cut through the fences at about 4:00 a.m. a red flare was shot up as a signal and the last fence was cut and all 80 commandos sprang into action. They overwhelmed two bunkers guarding the perimeter and poured onto the helicopter pad. Using suicide bombers and firing RPG 7's they destroyed 9 helicopters and damaged 4 more. Many of the CH 47 defenders were killed and the augmentation force was caught in an ambush.

By 27 February, the attacks fell off to nothing. The quick fizzle of the attacks puzzled some military analysts, but I believe the enemy was exhausted. Underfed and starving, they made one more attempt to take a military base or a provincial capital, in a desperate bid to quickly close the war. Failing to do so, I believe they just ran out of steam. Saigon was probably the ultimate target for these attacks. It always was, but in the interim, the capture of a provincial capital or the taking of Long Binh or Bien Hoa could have been a part of their game plan to force the United States to "sue for peace."

I served in Vietnam during General Patton's (then Colonel Patton) command of the 11th Armored Calvary Regiment (ACR). The unit headquarters was probably yards down the street from the 175th Radio Research Company (175 RRC).

While assigned to the intelligence section as a very young 96B20, I remember a request coming in from the field for a clarification. You know, us Intel types were sometimes suspected of giving out "funny" or suspect information. But the 175th RRC, which directly supported the II Field Force commander with intelligence, had a pretty darn good reputation for knowing what was going on and who we were up against.

Since this happened many years ago, I'm not exactly sure of the dates, but it was during one of the 11th ACR's battles along Highway 13 to open the road between An Loc and Loc Ninh. During this battle, the 11th ACR captured an NVA prisoner who claimed to be with the 101D regiment of the 1st NVA division. We had been watching the 1st NVA division move west and south and were perplexed at this development. If the prisoner was truly with the 1st NVA division, then the division had not moved at all, but was along highway 13 as well. The message sent to us from Colonel Patton was pretty direct and forward. He wanted to know what was up with that. He was informed that the 1st NVA division was nowhere near him and that he was only facing the 7th NVA division. If the 1st NVA and 7th NVA were both in his vicinity, then he would have to come up with some different strategic and tactical ideas. One US Cav Regiment versus two NVA divisions would provide him some problems.

We scratched our heads and began to look at our notes. Truly, the 1st NVA was leaving the area, so what was going on with the 101D regiment and the prisoner? It wasn't something that took a rocket scientist to figure out, but it was the first time I had seen a communist division switch regiments with another division in the field. From what I now understand, this was always in their doctrine, and this is what we told Colonel Patton. We figured the 1st and 7th NVA divisions either swapped regiments, or, the 1st NVA left the 101D behind to help with the battle, thus making the 7th NVA a "four" regiment division.

This seemed to satisfy Colonel Patton, and he thanked us in another message and gave us a pretty good pat on the back for a timely analysis of the situation. Of course, time proved us right. I took a lot of pride in that little exchange because of the great respect I had for the 11th Armored Cav Regiment and Colonel Patton. Truly, had I been a grunt, that would be the unit I would have chosen to fight with.

Chapter 12

BRINGING TOUR NUMBER 1 TO AN END–JUNE 1969 TO AUGUST 1969

In March of 1969, I was allowed to visit Australia for two weeks rest and relaxation. Australia was so different. To be English speaking and similar to us, they were totally different. When the plane stopped in Darwin, they came on board and confiscated all our girly magazines, unprocessed film, and other contraband material. Even though you could buy a *Playboy* off their shelves, you could not bring *your* magazine into their country. They also sprayed us down with a bug killer. Yep, sitting right in our seats, we were sprayed with a bug spray that killed all flies, mosquitoes, and other bugs we might have brought into the country. That was the most unpleasant thing the little short Australian customs man did to us.

We were not allowed off the plane, and after refueling we were off to Sydney. Landing in Sydney we were again met by a barrage of police and agents and herded off the plane to a holding room inside the terminal building. While inside the terminal building, we were given a list of different hotels we were allowed to stay in, I chose to stay in the King's Cross area.

We were finally released and I caught a cab with about three other GIs, off we went to visit King's Cross. At the hotel on the side of a hill, we checked in, and I was so glad to drop my stuff in a room that had two beds crammed into it. Yes, two to a room, but we didn't mind.

That afternoon I decided to go shopping and just looking around the department stores. The girls were gorgeous. I was wearing my brand-new blue shark skin suit I had made in Hong Kong, and I looked rather dapper. I wasn't really buying anything, just enjoying people who I trusted and who looked similar to myself. That may be a bit racist, but the truth is when you see nothing but Vietnamese women and men for a year, white or black, women with round eyes were just beautiful.

I was about to receive some life lessons at King's Cross, and it all began with a girl. A young girl, about my age or younger, was crying out-side a dress shop. I stopped and asked her what the problem was? She said if she had a new dress she could go to the local reception party I was invited to. So, I said how much is the dress? She said $60.00 Australian money. I said, "Well, I don't have a date for the party, so if I buy you the dress, would you meet me there?" She answered "Yes! That would be fantastic. Would you be so kind?" So, I went inside and bought the dress for her and gave her the receipt. We walked out, and she said, "Oh, thank you so much, so very much. I'll see you tonight." I told her I would be looking for her and my name was Ken. She said she would be looking for me.

I never saw her again. I expect what happened was as soon as I went around the corner, she prob-ably ran back to the store and returned the dress and got the money for it. That was a lesson learned.

The second lesson I learned occurred not far from the site of the first one, all on the same day. I visited a library some street hack was ushering GIs into. I followed him into the complex and found my way upstairs to a table of noise and excitement. Here was a man sitting with only three cups in front of him on a flat desk. Men were making bets and losing their money by the boat-load. I thought I had figured the game out, so I asked to try it.

The man agreed and put the pea (or very round bean) under the middle cup. I followed the cups around and around and around. I have very good reflexes and figured I've got this. When he stopped, he said $5.00 to make a guess. *Okay*, I thought, *$5.00 isn't that much besides I knew which cup that pea was under, it was under the cup to my right.* I paid my money, made my guess and lo and behold, it was in the cup to the left. "Again?" he asked. "Yes," I said. So I paid another $5.00 to play the game. Under the cup the pea went and round and round and round the cups went. I knew this time it was the middle cup. No doubt about it, I knew it. Well, it was under the cup to the right. *Darn it* I thought, *I know he's cheating, but how?* Eventually, after losing $25.00, I stopped playing. Bored of this game and losing money, I left for a burger and a milkshake.

That night I went to a night club in King's Cross, looking for my date. The club was built upward, like a five story building. The bottom floor had like reddish lights and a stage and a band. It was crowded and noisy. I asked where our party was located for GIs. I was told it was upstairs on the third floor. So, up the steps my buddies and I went, hoping to see this girl I had bought the dress for. All my buddies were pretty impressed I had a date already. On the second floor was a different band, dancing, and all the lights were blue.

Well, that was cool-looking, but we trudged up the stairs, yes stairs, to the third floor and all the lights were green. I thought this was very clever, and the floor was crowded with girls and GIs all dancing and what not. I looked and looked and looked, and finally I gave up. Chump was the term I heard. I had been taken. While it kind of upset me, I learned a valuable lesson that day about life. From brokenhearted women to slick-willy men, when it comes to money, they look for the easiest way to part you from your hard-earned dough. Lesson learned.

The next morning I was bored. I went down to the train station, and I bought a ticket to a place where I could visit kangaroos and emus inside their pens. I thought, *hmmm, this would be a really fun thing to do*. So, I bought my ticket for "Penn Hills" Australia, out near Richmond Air Force Base, not far from Ebeneezer.

The train ride was about two hours it seemed, maybe less. I was enjoying the outback, with scrub eucalyptus trees and grass, a real fire hazard. We made a lot of stops and one change at a siding whose name I have forgotten. I climbed on the next train for Penn Hills and arrived about mid-day. I caught a taxi from the station to the park and bought a ticket into the park.

I entered the park and was walking toward the kangaroo enclosure. You can only visit the little gray kangaroos because the red ones are big and mean. Grays are smaller and a little less aggressive.

I entered the enclosure and in front of me was a little old man who looked small and elvish in a way. He had a lady with him that I thought was his daughter. He was calling his pet kangaroo, George, to come to him. I watched in silence as he called "Here, George. Come on, boy, come see me. I have snacks for you." A small kangaroo came hopping up to him and stopped as if begging. He handed George a potato chip and looked up at me. "Hello," he said. "Would you like to feed him?" "Yes!" I said excitedly. He gave me the bag, and the kangaroo sat up for me, and I fed him another chip. "Go on, you can feed him." That's how I met Bill Cody and his sister. Bill was the ancestor of Buffalo "Wild Bill" Cody, so he said. Regardless, I spent an afternoon looking at animals with Bill and his sister. Toward evening, I said I needed to catch the train back to Sydney, but Bill talked me into staying the night with them.

Off we went in a small car to Ebeneezer, Australia. We stopped at an old church with an attached house. Both the house and church were connected with a portico. After a brief look inside the church, he took me into their house and I met other members of his family, including his wife and his niece. Bill's wife was fixing supper and had a nice table laid out. She quickly added another plate.

We sat down to a dinner of meat, vegetables, and bread, but no drink. I asked for a glass of milk. The look on their faces was one of utter shock. They don't drink and wash their meals down like Americans. Also, I was the only one who picked up a knife, cut meat, and laid the knife back down on the plate, across the plate. I ate with my right hand and my left hand tucked by my side, very mannerly. They ate with the fork in the left hand and knife in the right hand, very European.

I washed my meal down with milk, and we had coffee afterward. The niece asked me to show her something that was unique to America. I thought for a minute and I pulled out a dollar bill. I said, "Now watch what I can do with a dollar bill you probably can't do with other money." She watched intently, I put the bill between my two hands, holding each end with my index finger and thumb. I slightly brought my hands together and then pulled my hands apart "popping" the American dollar like a firecracker. She jumped, and they looked in amazement. Bill said, "Didn't that tear that bill apart?"

I said, "No, because it's got so many fibers in it the bill won't tear." I got a big laugh out of that, but the niece didn't ask for any more demonstrations.

I had a great sleep that night. It was so quiet and peaceful. I don't think I turned over once. I was dead to the world. In the morning, I had a big breakfast, similar to ours, and I had orange juice. We had a meal, then Bill said, "Ken let's go riding. I've got some places to show you and some friends I want you to meet. We'll make a day of it. What do you say?"

I said, "If it's not a bother, I'd love to travel out to Katoomba. It's not too much further west." He agreed and off we went on a road trip.

Now, some people might call what we were about to commence as "bar hopping." But, I would like to say it was meet-and-greet time in Australia. Off we went heading west toward Katoomba.

About five miles down the road, we stopped. "Got to see some folks in here" he said. With that we went into a pub and met a group of men and the bartender and his wife. I had a beer on the house, we talked for a bit, and Bill said, "Time to go!" and out the door we went, into the car and continued to head west.

We did this for about forty miles, stopping every ten miles or so at a different pub. I was about to get looped and asked him how did he know so many people. He answered that he did this on a regular basis, and that tonight we were going somewhere special. Finally, we reached Katoomba and visited the town a bit. Then we headed back to Ebeneezer, bypassing the bars (thank goodness), and stopping at a very large pub-restaurant type of place. We met the family there for supper and Bill introduced me to darts, a very serious game in Australia.

I played pretty good and didn't bet on any games. I learned my lesson. Then back to his cottage at the church, and we talked for a bit and I explained about the Civil War. They really didn't know how brutal the war was between the States. I think they wondered with that much war, how the country could ever mend itself. I explained the duality of being southern. I had confederate southern blood in my veins, yet very strongly patriotic to the United States. I don't think they got it.

The next day, Bill and his sister took me up into the Blue Mountains of Australia. We visited a place called Jenolan caves. It was an astounding underground world. The lighting in the cave was beautiful, and it was a stroll into the main cave. This was 1969, and the cave was a tourist location. It wasn't as built up or as well explored as it is today.

After visiting the caves, Bill drove me back to Ebeneezer where I caught a late afternoon train back to Sydney. I had one two-hour wait in some unknown spot along the railroad. Here I would catch another train for Sydney. When the train stopped, a few people got off and disappeared and left me alone on the platform.

Near me was a blond-headed man, a little shorter than me, but chilling out waiting on the train. It's my nature to try to be friendly. I said to him, "How are you? I'm heading to Sydney also."

He said, "I don't like Americans. I'm from Scandinavia." *OK*, I thought, *I'll leave him be*. I decided to keep to myself and just ignore him.

I had a long train ride back to King's Cross and my hotel room. I got to the room in the wee hours of the morning and slept in the next day. My buddy asked me what all had I seen, and I told him it was really quite a little adventure.

Soon we were back on a bird headed to Ton Son Nhut Air Base and eventually the 175th RRC. It was a good break. I could tell that my body was tired and I was out of steam. I was edgy and every rocket attack added to the stress.

In June 1969, I submitted paperwork for transporting a firearm back to the United States. I sent my paperwork, dated 19 June 1969, to the Department of the Army. I was an E4, specialist 4th class, when I submitted the paperwork. The rifle was a Chicom (Chinese communist made) Mosin Nagant Type 53, caliber 7.62mm. The serial number was C 7900 and it came off the battlefield outside Bien Hoa in February 1969.

I received a firearms export license from the Republic of Vietnam dated 1 September 1969. This allowed me to hand-carry the Chicom rifle back to my home in West Virginia. The Chicom Type 53 is a bolt-action rifle; it has no safety and is equipped with a flip-out bayonet. It fires a 7.62mm Russian

Short bullet. It remains in my possession as of this writing.

My time in the country was winding down. I was getting a little antsy. Even though I had volunteered for a second tour, I was ready to go home for a short break. Finally, August 1969 arrived, but before I climbed on that bird for the United States, a funny thing happened to me; I was summoned to a commander's call. I had just come off an all-night guard detail on the northern perimeter. I was tired, grumpy, and I had just climbed into my bunk. I was ordered up and to "get dressed and fall in or else" by my barracks sergeant.

"Or else what?" I quipped!

He was fairly ugly with me, "Or else I'll try to get you an Article 15. Now get up and get dressed."

Muttering to myself I got up, dressed, and fell in at the assembly outside the company CQ. I was immediately called forward with about a dozen other men, and we stood at attention in front of the company. I was awarded my first Army Commendation Medal this way, and was given a Polaroid photo of the presentation. I sent this photo home to Dad along with a letter that I wrote for Mom and Dad. Sort of my saying "Hey, this is why I extended for a second tour."

In that letter, I stated to Dad that I felt coming back over to Vietnam was important because I could help save lives if I did a good job as an intelligence analyst. I told him that my analysis had saved a few lives, and that I was good at it, and why shouldn't I come back instead of someone new who didn't know the ropes. In all honesty, February 1969 was burned into my heart and soul.

Dad put that letter into the newspaper, and the paper did an article on me and included the picture of me receiving the Army Commendation Medal. Truly it was not such a big deal, except to me, deep down in my gut, knowing that what I was doing was making a difference. Such as the time we predicted an attack against the 2/7th of the 1st Cav, and that attack occurred. Only several men were killed in that attack as the base was on full alert. This is where good analysis can save lives. It would be tested again later on in fall of 1969 and early 1970.

I returned home for a thirty-day rest before returning to Vietnam for a second tour of duty. I was very tired and worn out. I don't believe anyone realized how much was drained from me mentally and physically. It wasn't humping the jungle or dying in a firefight, but the stress of the importance of my job was real, the hours worked extremely long. We had no down time, except for the R&R we were given. I was losing that little voice God puts in your head, that voice that talks to you about things in life. The little voice that helps you grieve when someone dies or helps you enjoy a joyous moment, or helps you control your actions. That voice was disappearing and would go away for several years after Vietnam. I was going numb.

Chapter 13

BEAR CAT, HOME OF THE ROYAL THAI ARMY–1969

When my aircraft lifted off, the entire plane cheered. These men had survived a year in a combat zone and were finally leaving it. Most of them were leaving Vietnam for good; I was coming back. That was in my mind as we took off, a story not finished. The flight was long and tedious. We landed in Hawaii, and that was the first time I visited that state. The welcome was sweet; one that most of us remembered. The Hawaiian girls met us coming off the aircraft with a hug and a lei around our necks. From Hawaii to the continental United States was a long trip, landing at Travis Air Force Base in California. Here we were met by in-processing personnel where we were segregated. Those returning were shepherded to the part of the airport where we had waiting seats to fly back across the country. For most of this trip, I slept and sipped on sodas.

Arriving home, I was met by my family and got a great welcome home by my parents and brothers. I began to unwind a bit at home, but once, I let out a string of curses at someone on TV and I had to apologize to my Mom. She had never heard that language from my mouth. Later that week, Dad went with me to the Volkswagen dealer, and I bought a Sunset Red Karmann Ghia. I only had a learner's permit and did not have time to get my license. My dad or my uncle rode everywhere with me. I remember Dad taking me to St. Albans and making me stop on a steep incline. This is where I learned to use a clutch and gas pedal together.

While home, Dave, Carlos, and I, decided to hike up to the old Shupe house site, behind a neighbor's house up the other holler. There were four of us hiking this trail at night with a full moon. We didn't need a flashlight; the moon was so bright it lit the forest and open areas like a street light. We hiked further up the holler where we were out of sight of civilization. We were nearing an opening where a gas pipeline was installed. The open area was probably twenty or thirty yards wide. We started to enter the open area. There was a creek running beside us on the right side and a hill on our left side. As we approached the center of the opening, we heard hoof sounds coming down the path straight at us. All of us dove as the hooves went crashing by. When we recovered, I asked did anyone see anything? "No," was a unanimous reply. No one had seen anything, not a deer or a horse or anything. Just the sound of the hooves galloping past us. We had strewed gear all over the hillside getting out of its way, whatever "it" was. It's still a mystery today.

My family had a nice party and get together for me, and I remember many good things about that homecoming. My next homecoming in March of 1970 would be much different. I went through Fort Dix, New Jersey, on my way back to Vietnam. The day I landed in Philadelphia, rioters were burning down sections of the city. Clearly seen from the air, I thought about how the communists had infiltrated our culture at home. How insidious this cancerous type of government is and how it preys on the weak and the downtrodden. I shut it out of my mind. I couldn't function as a soldier and pay that a lot of attention.

We landed in Philadelphia, and I caught a taxi to Fort Dix. We were housed in World War II barracks again. It was cold. October 1969 in New Jersey was wet and rainy. On my first night at Fort Dix, we were given a guard mount in a dilapidated barracks area, barracks that were destined to be destroyed. I only had my jungle fatigues, no field jacket and no rain poncho. All of us were under dressed for this type of mission.

It started raining about 2:00 a.m. and after walking the beat for two hours, I was wet and freezing. I didn't have a change of clothes, either, except several T shirts. After that night of hell the next day the sergeant in charge started to line us up for roll call. We finally fell into line and answered roll call. When he started giving us commands to do a right face in preparation to march us to the chow hall, all fifty of us said, "Oh *no*! We aren't doing that" and we all walked off as a mob. He started to object, but someone reminded him that some in our company had killed better Viet Cong than he was. He shut up.

That evening I saw Robert Higginbotham, I think he was going back for a tour also. I can't remember, but it was great to see someone I knew from Nitro. We talked for a while and shook hands and parted. That made my stay at miserable Fort Dix a little happier. I only know one thing; I was glad to leave that place and made it a point never to visit that fort again.

My flight back to Vietnam was interesting. We stopped at Wake Island and heard the waves crashing on the shore. It was very dark, and the cantina and small gift shop were closed. I never knew that one of my distant cousins, Robert (Bob) Luikart worked there as a station master.

On my second tour in Vietnam, I was promoted to E-5, specialist 5th class, and was appointed the head of the intelligence section. I was back with my three intelligence analysts, Stan S., Patrick M., and a fellow from Texas whose name I cannot remember.

We began our transition from the old operations building to the new operations building. I often wondered why we built such a big building right on top of the hill, painted it white, added a double security fence around the building, and provided an MP shack out front to hand out limited-access identification cards when entering the building. Certainly, this should have been a prime target. But it was never hit by mortars or rockets, and it wasn't the target of a ground assault. I figured we were lucky; perhaps they just thought we fixed radios.

Shortly after the new building opened operations a group of visitors came sauntering through our work area. I don't know who they were, or where they were from, but I knew something wasn't right. After they had nosed through the ops area they were cornered and escorted off the premises. I am quite sure they were not cleared to be in our building. How they were allowed inside is a mystery to me. Probably good material for another book.

I was chosen to go set up an intelligence order of battle section at Bear Cat for a new detachment that was being established. Bear Cat was located down south of Bien Hoa and was the home of the 9th Infantry Division and other elements that supported the 9th Infantry in 1966. When I drove down to help set up a radio research signals intelligence shop in late 1969, Bear Cat was still the home of the Royal Thai Army.

Leaving Bien Hoa, I observed a long line of dog handlers, about fifty or so. Each dog was apparently happy to be out and walking on the highway. They were going out on a training mission. Bien Hoa was also where the dog handlers' school was. The sad thing about all of this is not one dog was brought back to the United States. After the United States pulled out, it was reported that all the dogs were destroyed by the ARVN. All those brave dogs were left behind to die, and I know their handlers were not happy to learn this.

Located just south of Bien Hoa and north and east of Saigon, Bear Cat was one of those small military bases that were cut out of the surrounding jungle. I wasn't used to the jungle being close to the perimeter; Bien Hoa had a killing zone on the northern perimeter that was probably a mile or two wide. At Bear Cat, it was tight; at least in my mind it looked that way. Driving to Bear Cat I remembered how Harold Biller was killed. Roadside bombs and ambushes were common. Bear Cat was smack dab in the middle of a lot of enemy radio hits, meaning our radio detections and listening equipment showed hundreds of radios in the area used by the Viet Cong.

Radio research (ASA) detachments relocated, and changed nomenclature, many times during the Vietnam War. It's sometimes difficult to put the pieces together, but I believe the unit I went down to support was the 335th Radio Research Company that relocated to Bear Cat on 28 August 1969. It was reassigned from the 9th Infantry Division at Dong Tam to the US ASA Group, Vietnam. (That was the 509th Radio Research Group.)

My days at Bear Cat were busy setting up an intelligence section. I showed the analysts how I created white order of battle tabs for signals intelligence locations and yellow tabs for collateral intelligence. I also explained to them how I used the ARDF (aerial radio direction finding) hits on a push-pin map board: black pins for Saturday, white for Sunday, red for Monday, and so forth. This helped to establish patterns. It was our way of using pins pushed into a map board for pattern analysis. Sometimes you would see a pin jut out eastward. Those were the first signs that perhaps an invasion was coming into the area from Cambodia. It was a useful tool.

Setting up the intelligence shop was hot and tiring work. We established a briefing map, briefing area, combat files, and other odds and ends that make an intelligence section click. We established their "destruction" policy as best we could. It was to pile it all up in the floor and go find a five-gallon can of diesel fuel. This policy would come back to haunt us.

Destruction of classified documents at the 175th Radio Research Company consisted a large furnace outside where all the Top Secret material was burned to ash. Emergency destruction consisted of two magnesium plates, one placed in the top drawer and one placed in the bottom drawer, and they were tied to an electrical plunger. From what I understand, the plates would simply melt the safe and its contents into a burning gooey heap. These plates were also used on board naval intelligence-gathering ships. Methods of destruction of classified information authorized during the Vietnam were burning, melting or chemical decomposition, pulping, and pulverizing. At Bear Cat, we had nothing but diesel fuel and a match!

On the first night after establishing the order of battle (OB) section at Bear Cat, the base came under a rocket attack, followed by a ground probe. During the attack, all files in the safe were pulled and dumped in the middle of the floor and prepared for destruction. After the attack, we spent hours putting all this stuff back into the safes. This happened about three nights in a row! The jungle was right up on the perimeter. There was no killing zone at all, there was the jungle, some fences, and the berm. This place was an easy mark for the enemy. I kept my rifle loaded and with me at all times. Usually I slept with my boots on. I didn't like running to the ops building barefooted.

It was at this point I had a great desire to return back to Bien Hoa and my magnesium plates. I wish we had those plates at Bear Cat. The newly created Intel section was getting on my nerves, not the ground attacks and rockets, but the continuous pulling out documents for destruction, and refiling them again.

Our return home was uneventful and the turn off of Highway 1 onto the road to Bien Hoa was like driving back into your old hometown. I actually had a good feeling seeing the gates of Bien Hoa again.

During my second tour, the army was busy trying to destroy the COSVN headquarters. In other words, we attempted to catch General Giap at a base camp and destroy him with a B-52 strike or artillery barrage. But there were many problems with this strategy and other operations in the III and IV Corps area of operations. Later I learned there was a huge flaw with this premise.

VC and NVA Headquarters' bunkers in the COSVN area were built with very large diameter, perhaps more than three feet, mahogany trees as roofs for the bunker. They were placed side by side as a roof covering and then buried under earth. A large bomb striking this facility above ground probably didn't do the damage we wanted. A lot of shock and destructive force was cushioned by the large timbers. I suppose one would have to be inside that complex upon impact to know for sure.

These are my reflections and do not necessarily agree with other analysts. That is the good thing about being an analyst and the worst thing about thinking things through to a conclusion. I did read General Giap's little book at the Air Command and Staff College. His book is about sixty pages. He explains how they won the war in sixty pages. General Davidson explains how we lost the war in about eight hundred pages. I think this might have been the real secret to the war. Giap's strategy was simple, and he used terrain and border features to prepare his units to strike into Vietnam. It was the premise for the US and ARVN invasion of Cambodia after I left the country. The problem with all operations involving large numbers of troops or aircraft is operational secrecy, and we had the worst operational secrecy of any army in the world.

I saw a document captured in 1969. This document had every single US Army infantry unit down to battalion level. They had every code word they used in combat for these units. They had all their code words for calling in artillery or aircraft. The Viet Cong were doing the same thing to us we were doing to them. It was an eye opener for me to learn how loose our communications were in combat.

B-52 strikes were usually compromised before the last aircraft left Guam or Thailand. The NVA had a B-52 watch alert unit. I figure it was a sampan working off the coast of Guam and perhaps a watch unit or units watching the aircraft leaving Thailand. First, they were listening to the B-52s talk to their operations center or to each other. Second, they were watching which way the aircraft made their turn at altitude. Yes, they were that good! They could alert COSVN, hours ahead of time, that the aircraft were coming to their area. COSVN would simply go deep underground, or they would move their headquarters as far away from the strike area as possible.

The Ho Chi Minh Trail was not really a trail. It was many, many trails with numerous crossing points across rivers. Some of these trails were even paved. Bombing the Ho Chi Minh Trail was fruitless. The jungle canopy and the numerous trails allowed the enemy to quickly move east or west as they needed to in order to continue the flow of ammunition, weapons, or personnel. So it wasn't one trail; it was hundreds. Along the trail, at river crossings, the NVA had established entire battalions of workers to repair bridges or key crossing points (fords). In addition, at these locations, the NVA had units that took the goods and men across the river to the far side and sent them on their way south. These people lived in the area. It was impossible to eradicate that capability.

The second feature that gave us fits were the base camps in Cambodia. COSVN was stretched between the Fish Hook and westward to the Dog's Head. In March 1970, the 1st Calvary Division and the 11th Armored Cavalry fought quite a battle in the Dog's Head area. That had to be a tough fight because it was practically dense jungle. Not an ideal place to use tanks or APCs.

South of there was the Angel's Wing, an area where a major highway pushes into Cambodia. This was another area where the enemy operated pretty much with impunity until the 1st Cav tried to cut off the enemy operating in the Parrot's Beak area. All of these landmarks are well known by many of the infantry men and troopers who pushed into the jungle trying to kill Viet Cong of the 5th and 9th VC divisions and 1st and 7th

NVA divisions. Each push is a special story, and many good soldiers performed many acts of valor in these encirclements. But to be honest, I think our own communications gave away our intentions way in advance. Because of the document that I saw, the whole schematic of how our units talk to each other was drawn out and studied and explained. We gave the enemy too little credit, and we thrashed about like a bull in a china shop, which is just my own opinion.

The number of rocket attacks and the enemy's constant surveillance of our base meant that the Viet Cong and North Vietnamese were still applying pressure to our base. Rocket attacks continued from 1969 to 1970 at Bien Hoa. One rocket hit very close to our hooch. Slamming into Lassiter field, it sent shrapnel throughout our hooch area. Nothing was hit, except a helicopter. I was able to pick up a piece of shrapnel as a souvenir, but it was confiscated as I was leaving the country in 1970 for good.

The bombing of Hanoi and North Vietnam was working. Stopping the bombing to appease the communists was playing into their hands. We were really upset by that move because we were still catching VC rockets at Bien Hoa. The communists argued for months about the shape of the peace table at the peace talks. I am not going into all that, but you can see they were stalling for time to organize and ship more troops south into the war zone. We knew we were hurting them, and we had killed quite a few soldiers in the two TET offensives. All the bombing halt accomplished was replenishment of those men lost by the 5th VC and 9th VC and 1st NVA and 7th NVA divisions. That's all it accomplished. We had them on the ropes; we were putting a real hurting on them. In addition, Uncle Ho Chi Minh died in late 1969, and that probably upset the apple cart a bit in their leadership, considering it was a dictatorship. In the grand scheme of things, I would have continued bombing until they quit, and I would have sought peace with the "South Vietnamese communists" (The NLF) instead of Hanoi. That would be the option I would have chosen. But then, I wasn't the president or the commanding general.

Chapter 14

VIETNAMIZATION–NIXON'S WAR– 1969 AND 1970

On my second tour of duty to Vietnam, from September 1969 to March 1970, I was involved in civil actions programs. The 175th Radio Research Company received five meritorious unit citations, one republic of Vietnam cross of gallantry with palm, and one republic of Vietnam civil actions unit award. The civil actions unit award was given for our work at the Bien Hoa Mental Hospital and the Ho Nai Orphanage.

Men volunteered to help work at both of these facilities as part of Nixon's Vietnamization. On steamy mornings or hot afternoons, men from the unit would climb aboard a deuce and half truck for a ride to the mental hospital or the orphanage. These rides would take you through narrow streets, crowded roads, past thousands of people scurrying past you in the Tam Heip, Ho Nai area and finally to the orphanage or the hospital.

The men that went to the mental hospital had a very tough job helping with hygiene of hospital patients forced to live naked in cells with small holes for feces and urine. The hospital staff would have our men go into the cell and help handcuff the patient, and hold him while the hospital staff washed him down and hosed him off. Then the patient was moved out of the cell while it was washed down with detergent and water.

Many of these patients were clearly mentally unstable; the war had driven them mad, and they were feisty and difficult to handle. That meant that they had to be handcuffed and held when taken out of a cell. Unit soldiers who volunteered for this assignment did not enjoy this task.

They complained of the smell of the holding cells, or living quarters. The soldiers complained that the hospital was overcrowded and nasty. It was not a favorite additional duty. Men seldom requested that duty a second time. The hospitals, especially mental hospitals, were overloaded. A five hundred-bed hospital may have as many as 1,500 patients. This resulted in overcrowding, nasty living conditions, and very disturbed and troubled patients.

I volunteered for the orphanage as often as I could. The ride to Ho Nai was across the main highway. Our unit provided materials and labor to a local Catholic orphanage. This work consisted of repairing broken-down buildings, installing a refrigerator, digging and installing a new sewage system, and procurement of building supplies. In addition, we procured clothes and toys for the children for Christmas celebrations in December 1969 and December 1970.

One of our projects was digging a new sewage line and installing a septic tank. Their well water was drawn less than ten feet from their slit trench latrine and a ditch for a water hookup. I'm sure the water was contaminated, but I never knew for sure. We dug a ditch for a water line some 100-plus feet to a water tie in. Soon the kids would have a flushing toilet and clean drinking water from a water spigot. It was hot the day we dug that ditch.

We had spent all day doing various other jobs and taking turns digging the water line. We were drenched with sweat, but all we had was our water jug with melted ice. The nuns brought us lemonade and pineapple slices. We balked at drinking the lemonade because of bacteria, but the nun assured us they had boiled the water and then added the ice. We all drank down at least two glasses each, not thinking about the ice. The ice must have been full of bacteria, and a day later, all of us were extremely ill. I was sick for two weeks, spending a lot of time on a toilet or a slit trench. My stomach was torn up, and to this very day, I still have a touchy stomach. I'm not crazy about spaghetti with a lot of sauce or cheese topping. I also shy away from ice cream, and though I love both, they just make me sick.

The unit finished the project and tackled another helping them organize their cabinet-building shop. I loved visiting the kids and pulling out a harmonica and playing different songs for them. Their favorite was "I've Been Working on the Railroad." The little boys needed father figures. You could tell they missed someone playing soccer with them or playing their games. And the little girls were just precious. I often wondered what happened to those kids after we came home. I wish I knew: Communists were very cruel to anyone associated with God, killing priests and nuns on sight or raiding Buddhist temples. Maybe the NLF kept them from committing atrocities. I'll never know. The 175th Radio Research Company carried this program on a voluntary basis. The orphanage was the Ho Nai Orphanage located at Bien Hoa, Vietnam.

At Christmas 1969, the children of Ho Nai Orphanage presented us with a little show inside our club. This was probably the highlight of my military career. Watching those little ones perform for us was inspiring and galvanized why I was fighting in Vietnam. The toddlers did a little dance with silk ribbons. The girls did a fan dance for us, and the boys did a stick dance. It was something that I will never forget. Afterward, we hosted a meal for everyone from the orphanage, and the little ones had American turkey, candied yams, and cranberry sauce.

One little girl at the orphanage particularly caught my attention. I asked my parents if they ever thought about adopting a little girl. I think they were dumbfounded, but they didn't say no. They just didn't have the money or a lawyer who could execute the paperwork. Little Hung was four years old, and she had one eye that was crossed. She was precious, polite, and a little doll baby. I went to Sister Suzanna and inquired about adopting her. She pointed out that many children were in the orphanage because the parents could not afford to feed them. Hung's father was missing and presumed dead, but the mother was very much alive and had children at home.

Sister Suzanna pointed out Vietnamese law prohibited adoption of any child who had a parent still alive. That squashed any hopes of adopting Hung, but I had care packages sent to me for her that had clothes and toys and other goodies, which I presented to her when I was over at the orphanage. She was a good little buddy and even though we didn't speak each others languages, we spoke to each other through mutual respect and love. This tempering of the soul reduced the hatred and ill will toward the Vietnamese. Except for communists, I backed off of my hate for all Vietnamese.

Years later, 1975 I believe it was, Mr. and Mrs. James Zeigler brought a family of Vietnamese over to their home in Rincon, Georgia. They housed them in an adjacent apartment to their home. The war was over, as the communists overran all of Vietnam. The atrocities were ongoing, and this family managed to escape and were granted asylum. Mrs. Zeigler reminded me the other day, in church, that I was one of the very few people who brought them groceries and gave them money to help sustain them.

Eventually they were able to get on their feet, and they moved on. My kindness and concern came from a deep, very deep, feeling of guilt for letting those people down and allowing communism to engulf the South Vietnamese. All they ever wanted was freedom of religion, freedom to travel, and freedom to raise their own crops. One can only imagine what suffering some of those people endured.

Chapter 15

FINAL DAYS OF MY US ARMY TOUR–1970 TO 1971

L ate in my second tour, a very strange attack occurred. I was preparing for the midnight shift, a twelve-hour shift that lasted until noon the next day. I was in the latrine shaving and cleaning up for work. At 10:00 p.m., three large explosions rocked the base. These explosions were incoming and were timed several seconds apart. They were much larger than a 122mm rockets.

I heard the siren go off, but there were no additional explosions. I made my way into the bunker anyway. As quickly as the attack began, it ended. I finished shaving and cleaning up and scrambled to the operations center. Here in ops, I was hoping to find out what had happened. However, the operations center was clueless. Some feared the NVA had brought a piece of artillery south near the base, but this was not substantiated by any evidence.

Phone and radio calls went out to all the units and detachments concerning what had occurred, but no one had a clue. Then at 2:00 a.m., three more shells hit the base, striking near the same coordinates and killing a total of three soldiers and wounding twenty.

Eventually, we found out the truth. An artillery unit of the ARVN 18th division shelled coordinates they were given for a harass and interdiction (H&I) mission. The unit of 105mm howitzers had no forward observer and were firing in the blind on coordinates given them by their higher command. An investigation was launched to find out if the person giving the coordinates may have been a communist agent working in the division. I never heard the rest of the story, but for three GIs, their deaths were senseless and irresponsible.

I spent six more months at the 175th Radio Research Company, visited Australia for a second time, and earned my second Army commendation medal. After I returned to the United States in March of 1970, I went to the West Virginia State Police Office to get my driver's license. I was twenty-two years old before I got my first civilian driver's license. The state policeman couldn't believe I had never had a civilian driver's license. When he found out that I had spent two tours in Vietnam, he signed the clipboard and gave me the paperwork. I didn't even start the engine for the required driving test.

In August 1970, I ordered a special license plate for my brand-new car, a 1969 Karmann Ghia. I wrote the governor of West Virginia requesting a special license plate number 1776 in honor of the birth of our nation. It was my way of continuing my patriotism. I received a letter from Arch A. Moore Jr., governor of West Virginia, dated August 6, 1970. It read:

"Dear Specialist Luikart: In response to your request, I am pleased to approve the assignment of special license number 1776 for a five-year period effective July 1, 1970. Glad I could help! Sincerely yours, Arch A. Moore, Jr."

I carried that number for almost twenty years. I have the last license plate number 1776 nailed to my shed wall. The special number was transferred and issued to my father's car after I moved away.

I finished my last nine months in the US Army as an instructor in the Department of Combat Intelligence, Order of Battle Section, US Army

Intelligence School, Fort Holabird, Maryland. I ended my time in the US Army on 22 January 1971.

After I returned home, there would be one large offensive in 1972, called the "Year of the Rat." The North Vietnamese sensed that the United States had reduced its combat forces to such a very low level that the remaining support troops could be overrun easily. Again, they miscalculated the combat resolve of US support troops and the South Vietnamese armed forces. Nixon's vietnamization plan had only one major flaw. Any plan that did not truly attempt to capture the hearts and minds of the people was bound to fail. That is, any plan that didn't keep United States Special Forces troops in close contact with the average Vietnamese citizen was going to fail. If you have ever watched John Wayne's *Green Berets* movie, you would notice that the SF guys actually lived with and ate the same food as the average Vietnamese. This policy was actually doing more to win the war than all the B-52 strikes in the world.

The problem was, we had thrown a "counter-insurgency" approach to the war away in 1964! Fortunately, we didn't make that mistake in El Salvador. Our Special Forces soldiers pounded into the heads of the El Salvadoran army soldiers: "You must win the hearts and minds of the people. That will cause the support for insurgency to dry up and go away." Liddell Hart, a great strategist, called this political and military move the "net laid over the population." Without providing loving care for the average Vietnamese citizen, the plans put forth by Johnson and Nixon were doomed to fail.

The United States forgot that this was an "insurgency" in the beginning, and by 1972 the "real Viet Cong," that is, South Vietnamese communists, had been eliminated by the North Vietnamese communists. The North Vietnamese leaders did not want any South Vietnamese communists giving him a hard time. Reports were coming in from the field that North Vietnamese and South Vietnamese communists were fighting each other over women, food, and other tangible things.

In the long run, the North Vietnamese prevailed because of a lack of resolve of our own country. We could have used that to our advantage by attempting to drive a wedge between the South Vietnamese communists and the North Vietnamese communists. From my point of view, we did not lose the war due to poor intelligence or fighting resolve. We lost it because the United States was looking for the "easy way out."

After the 1972 offensive, the United States stormed into Cambodia, upsetting the balance of power in that country. The result of that offensive forced Prince Sihanouk to step down and the madman Pol Pot to step in and take over Cambodia. The result of that US political and military blunder cost the Cambodians three million lives. Pol Pot, a Maoist type of communist (there are different types of communists), believed that everyone would be happy being a farmer, and he killed off everyone else!

The attack by the United States into Cambodia was a good idea that was poorly timed. That attack should have come in 1968 immediately after the TET offensive, instead of in 1972 when we were much weaker. However, weak communication security would compromise any US operation into Cambodia. I honestly believe they knew more about our operations and movements than some of our units in the field, all because of spies and lack of communication security.

Poor Vietnam, by 1975, they were left to stand on their own. During the Carter administration, the North Vietnamese sensed the United States would not come to the aid of the South Vietnamese. Using Cambodia as the jumping-off point, they overran the South Vietnamese and destroyed the South Vietnamese army, air force, and navy.

United States antiwar demonstrators, the clergy, and the churches, didn't even raise a whimper when the victorious North Vietnamese communists executed more than 200,000 South Vietnamese. If you go to Ho Chi Minh City today, you'll find most of your important bureaucrats are North Vietnamese communists. The South Vietnamese communists were either killed off in the 1968 and 1969 offensives or were eliminated by the North Vietnamese themselves.

When the North Vietnamese finally stormed into Vietnam in 1975, most of the traditional South Vietnamese communists were removed out of the way. So, the TET Offensive had two strategic goals. One was to take over any provincial capital and kill Americans, and second, to weaken the VC led divisions, and eventually remove many of the South Vietnamese communists and replacing them with North Vietnamese regular army troops.

The last great battle was fought by the ARVN 18th Infantry Division. They fought a retrograde defensive battle from north of Bien Hoa to Saigon, losing 66 percent of all their men in the fight. This Division showed real grit and determination trying to stop the communist onslaught. Their final battle is a story that deserves a book.

Back at home, I was sick. I had lost that little voice in my head, and I was lost. I went to my family doctor who treated me for deep depression. That made it worse. I had never contemplated suicide before 1975, but after that year I was not happy with myself. I was starting to suffer skin tumors and had a blood tumor removed from my left arm. I had skin nodules removed from my right arm and left arm. I was suffering from another attack of crotch rot. That was pretty much what it is – some type of fungus was attacking my body. Years later, a doctor in Savannah helped me overcome that malady, but I still have the fungus in my body.

My left inner ear is damaged from some outside force. My guess is it was caused by over pressure from the rockets that knocked me down and the 175mm howitzer barrages late at night without warning. Several times I had bunker detail in front of them, and they fired over our heads into some distant target miles away. The overpressure was tremendous and the noise deafening. A technician at a hearing clinic spoke to me in that "critical" type of admonition, "Why didn't you wear your hearing protection?"

I said to her, "Really? This was back in 1968, '69 and '70. I spent eighteen months in that environment. The Army didn't even have a "safety" officer in those days. Hearing protection? You've got to be kidding me."

It was after this disgraceful period in our nation's history that I felt a need to reenlist in the military. This time I chose the Air National Guard and served as an intelligence analyst. I served as the non-commissioned officer in charge (NCOIC) of the Intelligence office, and in 1979 I was offered a "direct commission" to 1st lieutenant in the Air National Guard. I maintained my traditional guardsman status until 1987 when I left my job as a forest technician at Union Camp and became the unit's full-time intelligence officer. Today I am retired as the vice commander of the 165th Airlift Wing Support Group.

The Grenada invasion, Operation Just Cause, and the Gulf War have vindicated the US military. In the long run, communism proved that it's a very bad form of government and cannot survive. I predict that by the time my children are my age, the communist Vietnamese government will die away, and some form of a democratic government will emerge.

Here are the facts from the Defense Casualty Analysis System (DCAS) as of April 29, 2008 concerning the deaths in Vietnam. These are not to be considered official records, but are as close as possible. You may draw your own conclusions.

Records on file as of April 29, 2008, concerning those killed in Vietnam.

7,243 African American

226 American Indian or Alaskan natives

139 Asian

349 Hispanic

229 Native Hawaiian or Pacific Islander

204 Non-Hispanic more than one race

49,830 White

58,220 Total

Of all casualties in Vietnam drafted or volunteered for Vietnam.

34,508 were regular (voluntary service)

17,671 selective service (drafted)

97 National Guardsman

5,762 Reserve

182 Not reported

58,220 total

Records show that 58,212 deaths were men
  8 were women
  58,220 total

Record of deaths by rank
  48,717 were enlisted men
  6,604 officers
  1,622 undefined
  58,220 total

By branch of service
  2,586 Air Force
  38,224 US Army
  14,844 US Marines
  2,559 US Navy
  7 US Coast Guard
  58,220 total
  (Defense Casualty Analysis System (DCAS) As of April 29, 2008 concerning the deaths in Vietnam.)

Additionally, there were more young men from West Virginia killed in Vietnam, per ratio of population, than from any other state in the Union. Officially, 733 men from West Virginia died in Vietnam.

Last, not one platoon, battalion, brigade, or division in Vietnam surrendered during the entire ten-year war. Most GIs fought to their death during ground attacks. Most figured they were going to die at the hands of their captors anyway. So, US soldiers fought hard, in dirty, ugly, rotting jungles. Some died doing their job, others died trying to help their buddies. It's easy to say the war was wrong or we shouldn't have been there. In my mind saying that cheapens the sacrifice of those that gave their lives, and spits in the face of their families left behind with nothing but a handful of medals and memories.

Was it worth it? Well, I remember my house girl asking me one time whether we were going home. I said, "Yes, some day we will go home."

"No, you cannot go home. The VC will kill us! you cannot go home!" I believe she knew more about the seriousness of our being there than we did. We did go home and left the Montagnards of the South Vietnamese highlands open to whole-sale slaughter. We left the religions of Catholic, Buddhist, and Cao Dai to their ability to deal with godless and ruthless communists alone. We left the average South Vietnamese who ran from North Vietnam to the retribution the communists decided to carry out against them. We left the soldiers and government officials to communist firing squads or prison.

It's almost unbearable to think of it, yet some probably don't care and wish all Vietnamese ill will. I'm not one of those men. I served at a very young age. Like most soldiers, being young has an advantage. You do not always understand or care about the danger. That's what youth brings to the battlefield. Becoming an E5 at twenty-one might be a little young. I thought I knew everything, yet I didn't have the seasoning age brings with it. Most of us were not married, and we were not buffed up like today's soldiers. We were kids carrying rifles, but on our own we found a way to grow up and face the enemy.

The enemy was brutal, mean, and seldom took prisoners. All of us realized we were probably going to be shot if we were wounded or captured. A worse fate would be captured and not shot. That would mean torture until death, or until you were condemned to die in front of some village audience by disembowelment and your entrails wrapped around you and the tree you were tied to.

While we made fun of the VC, we also had a deep-seated respect for his cunning and his resolve. It was a real war, up against a tough tenacious enemy. Sometimes the Vietnam veteran isn't given the credit due him. As Dave Breisch commented, "No VC fights to the death unless they are committed to the cause and believe in it." In their eyes, we were the ones invading their homeland, and we were the aggressors. The Vietnamese call the Vietnam War "The American War." Coming to terms with that now at my age is very difficult. I believed we were fighting to keep the South Vietnamese people free. Time has proven that communism does not work, and even the communists know this (David Breisch email, 2017).

I am not ashamed of my duty in Vietnam. I worked very long hours, and I know some of our work saved American GI lives. In the long run, I know that freedom and liberty are worth fighting for. I paraphrase Benjamin Franklin on freedom: if you are looking for safety and are not going to fight to become free, then you deserve neither freedom nor safety. In the long run, the Vietnamese failed to fight with all their heart for freedom. They sought safety instead. They ended as victims of communism. The bottom line is, they lost the war – not us.

I have to accept that and find a way to move beyond the guilt I felt after April 1975 when

Saigon finally fell. The ultimate slap in the face was calling it Ho Chi Minh City, a nice poke in the eye of all Americans that tried to keep the South Vietnamese free. Their failure to maintain their own freedom launched me into another military career in order to keep my sanity. I was fighting depression, remorse, and guilt. I wished that I had died in Vietnam and never had to face embarrassment and stupid statements they teach kids today. Suicide crossed my mind and always lurks in there waiting for a big failure to spring it back to life. I've fought off that urge with medicine, drugs, and God. After leaving the military with nothing to do and nothing to achieve, I felt useless.

I'm sure some teachers teach that the Vietnam War was immoral and a "wrong war" to fight. However, they should teach children that all war is wrong, and that a nation should seek a political solution first. By any means, short of giving the enemy something they are willing to bully us about if we go to war, we should go to win it or stay home.

Winning a war has necessary elements attached to the total war plan. A war plan begins with an "end state." If you don't know what you want the world to look like when the fighting is all over, then maybe you need to stop and take a hard look at what you are doing. There was no "end state" given to the undeclared Vietnam War. It was just a continuous drain on our nation and a fight just to be fighting, hoping the Vietnamese would pick up the slack and go win the war.

Today I look at our veterans of Iraq and Afghanistan who have had numerous deployments. Three or four or more yearlong deployments to a war zone burns out your force. I have noticed so many men that just had to retire early and get out, or just leave the services. They are burned out physically and mentally. I see the future of many of these veterans as balanced on the edge of a razor blade. One direction and they can fall into a more normal and useful life; tip the other direction and in about five years after their service ends, you will see suicides, drug use, and or drinking problems totally out of control. This is my prediction, hopefully it is absolutely wrong.

Today's enemies of the United States are capable of changing their tactics and techniques quicker than we can react to them. They understand the OODA loop (observe-orient-decide-act.) concept. Its why our current foes are capable of surviving in spite of our military operations. Their OODA loop capability operates quicker than our cumbersome system. By the time we discover their true capability and design Rules of Engagement (ROE) to operate under they have changed their tactics, techniques and weapons two or three times.

Finally, there are many more stories to tell about my thirty-three years in the Air National Guard, including the many countries I visited and the many operations I supported. It is ironic that my last war I supported was in 2003 and was called "Operation Enduring Freedom." I was the commander of the deployed Wing's Operational Support Flight (OSF). We supported C130H2 flying operations into Iraq and other countries. Moreover, I served as the liaison officer to the Omani Air Force. That was truly one of the most challenging jobs I have ever attempted in the military. But those stories and my life with my Boy Scouts and working for Union Camp are left to another day, and another book.

Epilogue:

HERE'S WHAT COLONEL TIN, NVA OFFICER, SAID—APRIL 1975

*T*he Wall Street Journal, interviewed former Colonel Bui Tin who served on the general staff of the North Vietnamese army. He received the unconditional surrender of South Vietnam on April 30, 1975. He confirmed the battle of the Tet 1968 was an American military tactical victory, but perhaps a strategic defeat. Here are excerpts from that interview:

Our losses were staggering and a complete surprise. Giap later told me that Tet had been a military defeat, though we had gained the planned political advantages when Johnson agreed to negotiate and did not run for reelection. The second and third waves in May and September were, in retrospect, mistakes. Our forces in the South were nearly wiped out by all the fighting in 1968.

It took us until 1971 to reestablish our presence, but we had to use North Vietnamese troops as local guerrillas. If the American forces had not begun to withdraw under Nixon in 1969, they could have punished us severely.

We suffered badly in 1969 and 1970 as it was. And on strategy: *If Johnson had granted Westmoreland's requests to enter Laos and block the Ho Chi Minh trail, Hanoi could not have won the war. . . . it was the only way to bring sufficient military power to bear on the fighting in the South. Building and maintaining the trail was a huge effort involving tens of thousands of soldiers, drivers, and repair teams, medical stations, communication units. . . . our operations were never compromised by attacks on the trail.*

At times, accurate B-52 strikes would cause real damage, but we put so much in at the top of the trail that enough men and weapons to prolong the war always came out the bottom. . . . if all the bombing had been concentrated at one time, it would have hurt our efforts. But the bombing was expanded in slow stages under Johnson and it didn't worry us. We had plenty of time to prepare alternative routes and facilities. We always had stockpiles of rice ready to feed the people for months if a harvest was damaged. The Soviets bought rice from Thailand for us.

And speaking of the treason in the United States: *Support for the war from our rear was completely secure while the American rear was vulnerable. Every day our leadership would listen to world news over the radio at 9AM to follow the growth of the antiwar movement.*

Visits to Hanoi by Jane Fonda and former Attorney General Ramsey Clark and ministers gave us confidence that we should hold on in the face of battlefield reverses. We were elated when Jane Fonda, wearing a red Vietnamese dress, said at a press conference that she was ashamed of American actions in the war and would struggle along with us. . . . those people represented the conscience of America. . . . part of it's war making capability, and we turning that power in our favor (Vietnam Insights; written by Colonel Bui Tin).

Colonel Bui Tin received the surrender of Saigon in 1975. He went on to serve as the editor of the *People's Daily*, the official newspaper of the Socialist Republic of Vietnam. Disillusioned with the reality of Vietnamese communism, Bui Tin now lives in Paris.

CPSIA information can be obtained
at www.ICGtesting.com
Printed in the USA
LVHW02s0301050618
579543LV00001BA/3/P